Doug Clark and Carol Bundy

The Horrific True Story Behind the Sunset Strip Slayers

Real Crime by Real Killers Volume 8

Ryan Becker, Nancy Veysey, and True Crime Seven

TRUE CRIME 7

Copyright © 2020 by Sea Vision Publishing, LLC

All Rights Reserved.

No part of this publication may be reproduced, distributed, or transmitted in any form or by any means, including photocopying, recording, electronic or mechanical methods, without the prior written permission of the publisher, except in the case of brief quotations embodied in critical reviews and certain other non-commercial uses permitted by copyright law.

Much research, from a variety of sources, has gone into the compilation of this material. We strive to keep the information up-to-date to the best knowledge of the author and publisher; the materials contained herein is factually correct. Neither the publisher nor author will be held responsible for any inaccuracies.

ISBN: 978-1731175410

Table of Contents

Table of Contents 5

Quick Note from The Author 11

I: The Twins 15

II: Careworn Carol 28

III: Gentleman Jack 37

IV: Dastardly Doug 53

V: Big City, Little Rock 60

VI: Melancholic Marnette 69

VII: A Short Story About Shannon 77

VIII: Confession Time 85

IX: The Cuckoo Cracks 92

X: Criminal Psych Consideration 103

XI: Inadmissible & Erroneous Evidence 111

XII: Trial & Error 120

Conclusion 136

Acknowledgments 145

About True Crime Seven 167

Explore the Stories of
The Murderous Minds

A Note

From True Crime Seven

Hi there!

Thank you so much for picking up our book! Before you continue your exploration into the dark world of killers, we wanted to take a quick moment to explain the purpose of our books.

Our goal is to simply explore and tell the stories of various killers in the world: from unknown murderers to infamous serial killers. Our books are designed to be short and inclusive; we want to tell a good scary true story that anyone can enjoy regardless of their reading level.

That is why you won't see too many fancy words or complicated sentence structures in our books. Also, to prevent the typical cut and dry style of true crime books, we try to keep the narrative easy to follow while incorporating fiction style storytelling. As to information, we often find ourselves with too little or too much. So, in terms of research material and content, we always try to include what further helps the story of the killer.

Lastly, we want to acknowledge that, much like history, true crime is a subject that can often be interpreted differently. Depending on the topic and your upbringing, you might agree or disagree with how we present a story. We understand disagreements are inevitable. That is why we added this note so hopefully, it can help you better understand our position and goal.

Now without further ado, let the exploration to the dark begin!

Quick Note from The Author

THIS IS NOT THE FIRST BOOK WRITTEN ABOUT the deadly duo of Doug Clark and Carol Bundy. It is highly unlikely that anyone will regard it as the best book about the couple dubbed, the "Sunset Strip Killers."

The couple's reputation has gained almost a cult-like status following the release of the television show, *Wicked City*, which was loosely based on the couple and their crimes. Although names and details were changed for the show, with this book, the authors attempted to stick to the known, verifiable facts, which will allow readers to draw their own conclusions.

No details were added, embellished, or imagined in a sensational endeavor to garner sales. All too often, "true crime" books are made up of material solely from the writer's own imagination or from "research data" gathered from Wikipedia and other unreliable sources. The authors sourced facts about the case from trial transcripts, police reports, interviews, and first-hand accounts from people who knew the accused, as well as the victims and their families.

One of the characters in this unfortunate saga was eleven years old when she became involved with the two adults whose criminal charges would make them infamous. Alternately referred to as either "Theresa" or "Shannon" in other sources, the author has chosen to use the name Shannon, when referring to her, and, although she is now an adult, her anonymity will be preserved.

As requested, some names have been omitted to ensure the privacy of those who were kind enough to share their stories and memories.

Discrepancies in dates and other data were noted during research, even within court documents and police reports. Where there were discrepancies regarding the spelling of a victim's name, as was noted more than once, the authors defer to the spelling the victim's family engraved on their tombstone, regardless of the way court documents recorded the spelling.

Although there were many murders police felt could be attributed to the same killers of Marnette Comer, Gina Marano, Cynthia Chandler, Exie Wilson, Karen Jones, Jack Murray, and a Jane Doe, there was not enough evidence to back up that theory.

The brutality of the crimes and condition of the victims, once discovered, are shocking.

Teen girls, not just stepsisters, but best friends, found murdered and dumped like trash.

A prostitute, who had arrived in California less than two weeks prior to her death, found decapitated. Her head would be discovered later after the killer kept it briefly as a trophy.

These and other crimes in this book occurred in and around Los Angeles, California, in 1980.

The reader will have the opportunity to decide if Doug Clark worked alone or in conjunction with Carol Bundy. Or had Carol Bundy been working alone the entire time? Had her fixation with Ted Bundy caused her to commit vicious assaults and murders just like the serial killer with whom she shared a surname?

Even more intriguing to think about: did Carol Bundy and her sometime lover, and later murder victim himself, John "Jack"

Murray commit the murders together to frame Doug Clark? Did Carol Bundy react as a woman scorned when Murray refused to end his marriage, kill Murray, frame Clark, who had also recently spurned Bundy, then in some form of guilty self-flagellation, confess to her part in the killings?

Two of those three possible murderers are already dead. Only Doug Clark remains, living on Death Row, professing his innocence.

The author has already drawn a conclusion. Now it is your turn.

Time to go back nearly forty years to when it all began; come along—if you dare.

I
The Twins

PAVEMENT THAT HAD BAKED IN THE SUN ALL DAY shimmered like the gossamer wings of a dragonfly as it lay radiating its heat up into the summer air—what little air could be found, that is. As the evening began and shadows lengthened, the stifling heat made the air feel heavy and oppressive. The demand on power plants due to an increase in electric fan and air conditioner usage threatened blackouts. Residents poured out of apartments, rundown houses, and cheap motels in search of some relief from miserable conditions.

If lucky enough to have a little extra money or the ability to hustle some up, the clubs and bars along the Sunset Strip offered parched souls cold drinks, musical beats, and air conditioning. There were plenty of people hustling on the strip in the summer of 1980. Some sold drugs, and some sold their bodies to obtain drugs.

There was a certain twisted symbiosis in the lives of those working the strip. They were integral to each other's survival while at the same time selling death via baggie, bottle, and body.

Keenly aware that their lives were in constant danger of being snuffed out, women still hustled their bodies for the drugs that gave them the fortitude to get out there and do it all over again, night after night. It was a vicious cycle of dirty needles, dirty customers, and dirty bodies.

Heroin abuse was waning a bit as the much cheaper drug crack moved into the streets. Crack did not require obtaining a needle or the even tougher task of finding a decent vein when years of use had left the user tapped out. Plus, it was cheaper. A twenty-dollar blowjob would enable a user to buy a couple of modest-sized rocks and keep them amped up for two to three hours. Crack was thought of as being "safer" by drug users since not having to deal with sharing needles meant less likelihood of catching hepatitis and other blood-borne diseases.

For the most part, up until the 1980s, STDs were largely made up of curable illnesses. Sex without a rubber might mean you had to get a shot of penicillin in the ass, but STDs were not generally considered deadly until the AIDS epidemic during that decade.

Violent robberies and assaults by people while on crack or in an attempt to score increased dramatically. The drug element was something most working girls understood the dangers of, but being stalked by serial killers was not. No year before, nor since 1980 has seen more homicides in America.

As record summer temperatures soared and lingered around the triple digits, so did the number of crimes committed. California easily led the nation in crime, particularly violent crimes against individuals, namely rapes and murders. It was a deadly decade when the Sunset Strip murders occurred, and at the time, it seemed serial killers were crawling all over California.

One of the saddest things about the story of the first two victims, to me, is that they have consistently been labeled as prostitutes ever since their death; however, no proof is yet to be found, which indicates there is any truth to that. The only person to insinuate that either girl was involved in prostitution was the person convicted of killing them: Doug Clark. Gina Marano—

often misspelled as Narano in both news articles and even a few court documents—aged fifteen, and Cynthia Chandler, sixteen, were not just stepsisters—they were best friends.

Although born on opposite coasts of the United States, the sisters had grown so close that perhaps it makes sense that distance did not separate them at the time of their deaths. Gina's father and Cynthia's mother had married and moved their respective children to Huntington Beach, California, to live as one big, blended family. Both girls made friends easily, were bright students capable of doing well academically, but like a lot of teens, they seemed to resent what they perceived as restrictions on their freedom imposed by their parents. The girls had a history of running away from home, occasionally ending up in Cynthia's place of birth: Los Angeles.

While most people arrive in Los Angeles seeking wealth, a great many, especially young people, arrive seeking something entirely different—excitement. Gina, a beautiful brunette with olive skin, and Cynthia, a lovely blond with a sun-kissed glow, were among those looking for excitement. It was not unusual for males and females alike to hitchhike during the 1970s and even into the 1980s. "Stranger Danger" was a slogan still a few years in the future.

Stepping into a car with a stranger was dangerous, but it was also a common occurrence, and the two girls presumably felt there was safety in numbers. As they thumbed their way along the coast, the girls generally kept to the busy freeways where they were more likely to be offered a ride, and they always stuck together.

The sisters' bodies were found on June 12, 1980, not far from a California highway off-ramp. It appeared to the investigators that the girls had been killed at another location and their partially nude bodies dumped from a vehicle and rolled down an incline, where they came to rest amongst desert scrub and brush that reached upwards to the unforgiving sky. No attempt had been made to conceal the bodies.

The bodies of Gina and Cynthia were dumped in a similar manner and location as some of the victims attributed to the "Hillside Strangler;" however, Kenneth Bianchi and Angelo Buono, the two cousins arrested and charged with the murders, had been off the streets and in police custody since January 1979, which made it impossible for the two girls to be victims of Bianchi and Buono.

The girls had been murdered at some point the previous day, only a few hours before their bodies were discovered. The sweltering California heat, however, had already caused the bodies to bloat, and decomposition was progressing at a rapid rate. Skin that had once glowed with youth now held a waxen pallor and threatened to burst open as it was stretched taut from the gases created by the process of decomposition.

Around one in the afternoon on June 12, a worker clearing debris and litter in the area near Forrest Lawn Cemetery found Gina's body lying face down and Cynthia's body a few feet away. Gina's clothing had been removed except for the red tube top she was wearing, which had shifted down to her waist. Cynthia was still partially clad in a pink jumpsuit, which had been slit up the leg with a sharp instrument, all the way to the crotch.

Neither girl had on panties, but it was not readily apparent to officials at the scene whether any sexual assault had occurred either prior to or following their deaths. Except for the girls' clothing being partially removed, torn, and in disarray, there was not much evidence of this being a sex crime.

A small amount of blood and a drop or two of what was believed to be motor oil was noted on Cynthia's jumpsuit. Gina had succumbed to gunshot wounds to the head, while Cynthia had, in addition to a matching head wound, been shot in the chest at close range. Black burn marks, which fanned out in a speckle pattern, told investigators that the muzzle of the gun was either held extremely close to or pressed into Cynthia's chest.

Finding very little of any evidentiary importance, investigators nonetheless collected any stray cigarette butts, beer bottles, or paper wrappers—anything that might assist them in finding out who was involved in the girls' deaths. Police faced the grim task of not only identifying a killer but identifying the victims as well.

At the time of discovery, neither girl was found to be carrying an identification card on her person, which resulted in the necessity of both being given Jane Doe monikers until family members came forward and were able to identify them as their loved ones. The girls had been dumped so casually, and with such disregard for human life, it seems doubtful that this would have been their murderer's "first kill."

The perpetrator seemed comfortable with killing and handling the bodies. Cynthia's body displayed marked lividity; a phenomenon caused by the cessation of blood circulation when the heart stops beating at the time of death. Blood, which would normally be in constant motion, propelled by the natural pumping action of the heart through the various blood vessels, becomes dependent on the force of gravity, pooling in the areas closest to the ground.

It was this lividity on Cynthia's body and the lack of any blood at the scene that told law enforcement the girls had been killed elsewhere and transported to the area in which they were found. Police cordoned off the area with yellow crime scene tape, although it would not deter the only living creatures in the area—insects setting up house and making meals from the remains.

Gina and Cynthia's parents were looking for their daughters the day the bodies were discovered; they were able to identify them and give police a bit of information and insight. Gina's father recalled talking to his daughter a week or two earlier but had not heard from either girl since. Right before the girls' murders, they had been at a party in Beverly Hills where they had been introduced to a girl by the name of Mindy Cohen.

Cohen, a nineteen-year-old from an affluent background, was a very down-to-earth type taking an interest in the two girls who seemed so out of place at a catered affair in the hills. Cohen was able to fill in some of the missing pieces for authorities concerning the days surrounding the sisters' deaths.

Cohen's boyfriend, thirty-eight-year-old Mark Gotteman, was a wealthy lawyer who loved to party and threw hedonistic drug-fueled fêtes with guests ranging from business professionals and people in the entertainment industry to strippers and prostitutes. Gotteman had a close friend named Richie, who owned a long, sleek limousine driven by a tall, handsome chauffeur. This chauffeur was often sent out by his boss in search of attractive girls to bring back to the Gotteman mansion to party with other guests.

Allegedly, a few nights before the girls were killed, Richie dispatched his chauffeur and limo on just such a mission, and while cruising slowly down the Sunset Strip, the man happened across Gina and Cynthia. He brought them back to the mansion with him. In her statement to the police and the testimony she gave at trial, Cohen said she quickly struck up a conversation with the sisters. Gina told Cohen they had gotten jobs at a Taco Bell near the place they were currently residing, but if they were employed, Cohen thought to herself, it was obvious that they were barely getting by. Despite the girls having a hungry look about them, as if they weren't getting enough to eat, Cohen envied the girls and their bravery in striking out on their own.

She might not have been so envious had she known what neither sister had told anyone, that Gina had been drugged and raped at a party a few nights prior to the one at Gotteman's mansion. Cohen gave Gina her name and phone number, which she had written on a piece of paper, urging them to call her day or night if they were ever in trouble or needed anything.

Gina kept a red address book with her at all times, and she stuck the paper in amongst the business cards and notes already in it. Gina's father spoke with the police about his daughter's address book, but it was not at the scene, nor was it ever recovered.

Mindy Cohen had more to share with the police. She contacted police in a terrified state after receiving a phone call from a man who identified himself as a police detective. After introducing himself, he went on to say that he was investigating the deaths of two teen girls with whom she was acquainted—Gina Marano and Cynthia Chandler.

Cohen's number had been found in an address book one of the girls had with her when the bodies were discovered, the detective told her. He asked if it would be possible to come by and ask a few questions, but Cohen's parents were out of town, and she was babysitting her younger sisters. She gave this as her reason for not meeting with him that day, but she was willing to answer any questions the detective had.

After a few seemingly inconsequential questions, the man claiming to be a detective with the LAPD asked Cohen if she knew the girls had been prostitutes. No, she replied, she had not heard anything about that. The police had confirmed this, the caller informed her, because a man's business card had been found with one of the girl's bodies, and the man admitted to paying the girl for sex.

It was only after Cohen hung up the phone that she realized she could not recall the name the detective had given her. She also thought it was highly unusual for a police officer to go into so much detail about what was still an ongoing murder investigation. The thought of him telling her that the girls were prostitutes as if he felt the need to convince her it was true, made her uncomfortable. While thinking over the phone conversation, Cohen realized she had told the caller she was alone in the house with her younger sisters because her parents were out of town.

Now she wondered, not only if this could have been Gina and Cynthia's killer posing as a cop, but if he had her address as well as her phone number. If she had known that Gina's address book had not been at the scene, she would have known that her feeling that it had been the killer on the other end of the phone was correct. In tears, she called her lawyer boyfriend, Mark Gotteman, who, in turn, placed a call to the LAPD. No one from the precinct had made a call to Cohen, they told him; it must have been a crank call. Nevertheless, Cohen and Gotteman were worried.

A few days later, a woman by the name of Laurie Brigges also received a call from a man claiming to be a detective with the LAPD, who had been assigned to the Marano-Chandler investigation. Brigges' husband, Henry, and his brother ran a moving company, and Henry had been one of the last people to see the girls alive. Henry's business card was found with the girls' bodies; the caller stated—the same type of story that Mindy Cohen had been told. Laurie asked if Henry should call or come down to the station to speak with the detective, but he assured her that it was not necessary, and they would be in touch.

When Laurie relayed the message to Henry later, he told her that on June 11, he and an employee had seen the two girls. The girls had been hitchhiking, and the men were worried about their safety, so they had given them a ride and warned them of the dangers of hitchhiking. Brigges had given the girls his business card and said that if he could help in some way, to call the number listed on the card. He never saw or heard from them again.

Upon reflection, Henry decided it would be best for him to contact the police and offer any information he might have that could assist them in capturing the killer. As with Cohen's experience, the police said no one had called the Brigges' home and to disregard the phone conversation as some type of prank.

Henry Brigges agreed to try to put the incident out of his mind, but he couldn't forget what had happened to the two sweet girls, and Laurie couldn't forget the sound of the caller's voice. Even the blistering California sun couldn't rid her of the chills she got when she remembered it. It sounded like pure evil.

II

Careworn Carol

Less than a year after the United States was attacked by the Japanese and subsequently entered into World War II, Carol Mary Peters entered the world. Born August 26, 1942, to parents Charles and Gladys, the newborn was so lovely. The parents were sure she would grow to become a beauty, just like her mother.

When Carol was three years old, her sister, Vicky, was born, and this event seemed to coincide with major changes in both Carol's outward appearance and her outlook on life. As Carol grew and entered into her school years, the girl who once possessed a sweet and sunny disposition and precious baby doll looks, evolved into a sullen and withdrawn, overweight child.

Fate dealt her another cruel blow by the necessity of wearing large coke bottle glasses to help correct her poor vision. Teased and taunted by classmates and shunned by her own siblings, Carol retreated into a literary world of make-believe, devouring title after title of science fiction and fantasy tomes.

Carol arrived home one day after school to find the door locked. Pounding on the door and calling out for her mother to let her in until she wilted to the ground in tears. At last, she heard what she knew to be the sound of her mother's voice from inside the house, even though it was obvious Gladys was trying to disguise her voice. "Go away, little girl," the impossibly high soprano voice called to Carol. "You don't live here anymore."

The fact that Carol's siblings did not remember events the way Carol stated they happened could be an indicator that Carol had invented them or that children interpret and recall events differently. An item not disputed by anyone is that both parents were alcoholics and prone to violence. Carol was eventually let back in the house. Despite the harsh memories she had of her mother,

Carol related that she was panic-stricken the day her mother suddenly paused mid-sentence as her face turned a chalky white.

Carol, in tears, pleaded with her mother asking what was wrong, as Gladys slowly made her way to her bedroom to lie on the bed, she told Carol to go get her father and tell him she was not feeling well. Charles immediately left work, and gently scooping Gladys up in his arms, took her to the hospital. Charles returned home alone long after dark, and through tear-filled eyes told his two young daughters that, despite the doctor having given their mother a shot—adrenaline or lidocaine, which are used in certain cases of cardiac emergency—their mother had died.

Losing the mother, who had never been particularly loving and nurturing to Carol, would still leave a void. There would never be any reconciliation or chance to work on establishing a better mother/daughter relationship. This would lead to several toxic relationships in which Carol saw herself as both the alpha, who was in charge of doling out affection, and the downtrodden submissive constantly seeking attention and acknowledgment.

The void that Gladys' death had left was a topic her father, Charles, broached with both daughters almost immediately, according to Carol and Vicky. Gene, the eldest Peters child, had already left home by the time their mother passed away. Charles made it clear that his daughters would be expected to take their deceased mother's place in every aspect—including her place in the parental bed. Carol, thirteen, and Vicky, eleven, had no real concept of what adults did in bed, but they knew that the idea of being alone in bed with their father terrified them.

Charles did not care which one of his daughters accompanied him to bed that night, he informed them, just make a decision and be quick about it. Carol and Vicky played a game of rock-paper-scissors, with the loser being required to follow Charles into the darkened bedroom. Carol's relief at Vicky for being the loser was quickly replaced by fear for her younger sister. She pressed her fists as hard as she could against her ears in an attempt to block out her sister's cries and the sound of her pleading with Carol to come and help her.

The guilt that began growing inside Carol that night would stay with her for many years. She felt she should have offered herself to their father so that eleven-year-old Vicky would not have to experience the loss of her innocence and virginity only hours after their mother's death. Charles initiated both his daughters into the adult world of sex. The abuse continued for the better part of a year until their father met and married a woman and moved her in.

Carol was acting out in dangerous and disturbing ways. She developed an interest in voyeurism and would often watch neighbors outside their bedroom window. Carol, having been introduced to sexuality so young, would often streak naked through the neighborhood at night and masturbate openly outdoors, progressing to trading sexual favors for small amounts of cash. Offering her body to classmates and a school bus driver helped Carol find some of the attention she so desperately craved. She never enjoyed the physical act, but adored the feeling of being desired, no matter how fleeting.

Caro began running away from home when Charles was at his drunkest and most abusive. Returning home one evening, Carol was surprised to find no one there, and the case for her father's shotgun was lying empty on the floor. Slowly scanning the dark living room with her poor eyesight, Carol noticed the curtains were torn, and there were spots of what, on closer inspection, appeared to be blood. That was when she saw the family cat, dead from a shotgun blast that had rendered its small body nearly unrecognizable.

Her father appeared at the door, and in an oddly calm and detached manner, Charles told his daughter he had become enraged while arguing with her stepmother and made a swift decision that he would murder his entire family, starting with his wife. Realizing her husband's plans and knowing his penchant for violent acts, Carol's stepmother was able to wrestle the gun from Charles, but not before a random shot was fired, killing the cat.

Charles's wife, understandably, filed for and was granted a divorce and never returned to the Peters house. Custody of Carol and Vicky was remanded over to foster care, where they were shuffled around before being passed on to a grandmother in Michigan and an uncle who lived in Indiana. Less than a year after his attempt at exterminating his family, Charles made the long journey from California to Indiana and brought the two girls back to live with him.

At the age of seventeen, Carol decided she could no longer tolerate the daily beatings she was receiving from her father and his drunken tirades. She married a fifty-six-year-old man she did not love, who was also an alcoholic. Leonard, her husband, turned out not only to be an abusive drunk but also refused to hold down a job.

At seventeen, Carol lacked the education and work experience that would enable her to support herself and her husband. Leonard came up with what seemed to be a simple solution; Carol should use what knowledge and experience she had to support them by becoming a prostitute. Sick of his drinking, abuse, and insistence that she sell her body, Carol fled her husband just as she had fled the abusive drunkenness of her father.

Meeting the next man in her life, Richard Geis, could have been the turning point in Carol's life, a point where she made something of herself. Geis was a writer, specializing in pornography, with the occasional foray into the genre of science fiction. Carol was transfixed by the idea of earning a living as a writer and had secretly harbored a desire to be a writer or artist. Geis encouraged Carol's attempts at writing. He gave her a typewriter, a crash course in writing, and pushed her to sell her work. Carol was able to sell some articles and even wrote, illustrated, and published a single edition science fiction fan magazine.

Though she was gifted with writing as well as artistic talent and had found a person who gave her the emotional support she missed out on during her life, she soon gave up. When Carol was twenty, she received word that the man who had tormented her for two decades was dead. Her father, Charles Peters, had hung himself. Carol pulled the blame for his death around her like a familiar blanket.

Entering a stage in her life devoted almost entirely to a fruitless and vacuous search for someone to care for her and take care of her. Any slight by a lover sent Carol emotionally back to that scared child who craved love from the very people she feared. Carol often used the smallest excuse to run and to break things off with a partner before the relationship began to sour or before they could dump her first.

Geis and Carol continued seeing each other, despite obvious signs that this was not a forever pairing; a realization Geis came to once he learned Carol was still having sex with men for money. It was Richard Geis who paid for Carol to attend nursing school, and in 1968, Carol's life seemed to be finally shaping into something with real possibility. Hope blossomed and bubbled up within Carol.

Even as she and Geis parted ways as lovers, they remained lifelong friends; he was someone Carol would continue to call upon in times of crisis. One of the things Carol was most hopeful about as she ventured forth into her new role as a healthcare provider was the new love interest in her life. A healthcare provider named Grant Bundy. He and Carol initially seemed to get along quite well together, but when Carol became pregnant with the first of the couple's two children and began developing health problems, a death knell sounded on the relationship.

Carol, a diabetic, had always experienced difficulties with her vision; with two young boys, Carol was not taking proper care of herself, and her vision worsened. Grant worried that it was due to her diabetes and developed a fear of Carol becoming completely blind and rendering her unable to work, leaving not only the entire burden of providing for the family solely and squarely on his shoulders, but the care of both children and Carol would be left to him.

Grant became increasingly violent, and with flashbacks of prior relationships and her father's frequent beatings screaming in her head, Carol left with her two young sons and took refuge in a battered women's shelter in January 1979. She had no way of knowing at the time that this new beginning would also signal the end.

III
Gentleman Jack

JACK MURRAY ARRIVED IN CALIFORNIA WITH dreams of becoming even more famous than Tom Jones, the beloved singer with whom he was so often compared.

Born and raised in Australia, Jack reveled in the persona of a rugged gentleman from the outback. His manner, at first charming, took on a more Mr. Hyde-type after a few drinks.

A consummate liar, Jack told tall tales of every kind. Jack was known to carry a police badge to back up his claims of being associated with law enforcement.

This was a point Doug would make when Cohen and Brigges both stated in court that he was the person who had called them, impersonating an LAPD detective. It was Jack Murray, Doug told the court, who enjoyed impersonating a police officer.

Jack and his wife Jeanette were raising their two children in an apartment complex they managed called Valerio Gardens, and at night, Jack would moonlight as a crooner at country-western bars—most frequently one called Little Nashville. The outward appearance of a gentleman with a gentle spirit was shattered as soon as anything angered him—and he was quick to anger. Careful to present himself in the best possible light when meeting women, he rapidly progressed to a sadistic abuser.

Jeanette was aware of her husband's dalliances with women he met at the bars he performed at, as well as women who lived in the complex. She was quiet on the subject as she had suffered plenty of black eyes and even a broken arm at the hands of her husband and did not want her children to witness the abuse.

Jack was literally capable of charming the pants off women and carried on numerous short-lived flings. He implemented the same psychological tactics as Doug Clark. After showering a woman with attention and playing the role of a caring lover, he would then become aggressive and use sadomasochistic acts to frighten the women and assert his dominance. He had become so frenzied on one occasion that he'd torn his lover's nipple off with his teeth.

Jack enjoyed the role of leader, and his managerial duties at the apartments suited him just fine. When he met a dumpy, nearly completely blind thirty-seven-year-old divorcee who was searching for an apartment in 1979, he arranged for her and her two young sons to move into an apartment best suited for her disabilities. Ensuring that tenants had access to basic needs and assisting them in acquiring things such as secondhand furniture for their dwellings, he had cemented his place at the top of the Valerio Gardens hierarchy.

Jack's favorite topic of discussion was himself, and the shorthaired, dowdy new tenant was so desperate for company that she welcomed his visits and listened intently to his stories and delusions of grandeur. Topping off his drink at frequent intervals, it was not long before Jack Murray was drunk, and Carol Bundy was smitten. They drifted into the bedroom and began their twisted affair of sadomasochism and perversion.

Jack encouraged Carol, who had been told her blindness was irreversible and progressive, to seek a second opinion. He also took her to sign up for disability. She received retroactive payments and began to receive a steady check each month. The second opinion brought good news as Carol was told she had cataracts, which would be possible to remove in two separate operations. After the operations, Carol had been pleased to see so well again but disappointed at the image in the mirror that she was now able to see so clearly. On what would be the first of many such occasions, Jack used this opportunity to make Carol feel obligated to hand over cash.

If Carol was hesitant handing over cash, Jack quickly reminded her that, without him, she would not have the money in the first place. Along with Carol's disability payments, Jack had also made sure that when the house she owned with her ex-husband, Grant Bundy, was sold, she would receive her fair share of the profits. During his nonexclusive affair with Carol, Jack managed to convince her to use fifteen thousand dollars, a combination of money from the sale of her house and social security checks, to open a joint account in both their names, as well as providing him with huge lump sums of money at his request.

One of the lowest and most despicable plots Jack used was telling Carol in a tearful voice that Jeanette had been diagnosed with cancer, and an expensive operation was needed if she stood any chance of surviving. Choking through his sobs, Jack said he loved Jeanette, even though he had done her wrong, and he couldn't imagine telling his small children that their mother was dead, because he couldn't get her the surgery she needed. Carol was now in tears. Anything he needed, she said, she would give him anything. She gave Jack the requested ten thousand dollars without hesitation. Jack smiled and wiped away the crocodile tears. It had worked like a charm.

Around Christmastime, Carol made a desperate bid to spend time with Jack, hoping he would realize how much he cared for her and enjoyed her company. She planned on paying for a trip for the two of them to Las Vegas. While there, she would explain to Jack that she could offer him everything he needed and seemed to be lacking in his marriage to Jeanette.

Jack agreed to the plan, instructing Carol to leave with her suitcase separately so as not to arouse suspicion. The first night in Vegas, the two ate dinner together and took in a show. Jack then promptly disappeared, leaving Carol alone. She did not see him again until it was time to depart for the airport and their return flight home.

Carol rode back from the airport with Jack in his van and sulked the entire ride back to Valerio Gardens. Arriving at the complex, the two had a bitter exchange, and Carol fled to her apartment. A short time later, someone knocked at her door, and the ever-optimistic and delusional Carol believed it was Jack coming to apologize. Swinging the door wide open, prepared to forgive Jack for everything he had done, she instead found Jeanette standing on her doorstep with both of Carol's suitcases. Carol had been so upset when she fled the van that she had forgotten her bags were still in it.

Jeanette told Carol she wanted her to leave Jack alone. She was aware that Carol made up excuses for Jack to come to her apartment to fix things she had broken intentionally. The entire complex, Jeanette informed Carol, was talking about the way she followed Jack around and made cow eyes at him. She was making a fool of herself and should try having a little more pride, Jeanette told her wearily. She was tired. Tired of Carol chasing Jack. Tired of Jack screwing around behind her back. Tired of it all.

Carol was not certain that Jeanette knew she was carrying on an affair with Jack the entire time she had been living at Valerio Gardens, but she believed Jeanette had a suspicion at the very least. In addition to all the money she had given Jack and the presents she had bought him, she had given him a video camera and VCR for Christmas. Both were expensive gifts, and she was not sure where he had told Jeanette they had come from. It was this video camera, in fact, that Doug would attempt to have entered into evidence, alleging it had been used by Jack and Carol to record their crimes, which they would then sell on the black market as snuff films.

This was a story that echoed the crimes of serial killers Leonard Lake and Charles Ng, who together kidnapped women to use as sex slaves. The duo would videotape the tortures, rapes, and murders of their victims. What Doug did not mention, however, was that, just like Lake and Ng, he had often fantasized about having a place in which to house and torture women he had abducted.

Thinking about the money she had given to Jack made Carol remember Jeanette's alleged poor health and the surgery she had required. Carol inquired about Jeanette's condition and whether the operation had been a success. Jeanette put the pieces together and informed Carol she had never been diagnosed with cancer. The entire story must have been a ruse by Jack to get money from an easily manipulated Carol Bundy, she said.

Carol offered Jeanette fifteen hundred if she would divorce Jack. It was the final straw for Jeanette, and she demanded that Jack order Carol out of the apartment complex.

Jack found an apartment for Carol and the boys, which was far enough away that he would not have to see her unless he chose to do so. It was also conveniently close enough for him to drop by when he wanted money or sexual favors. On the day Carol moved in, Jack helped her with moving her furniture and other belongings. Jeanette followed as well, parking a short distance away to ensure there were only moving vans and no roaming hands that day.

Carol and Jack's relationship continued to unravel, and Jack had even begun ignoring her when she showed up at Little Nashville, hoping to catch his attention. It was on one such occasion that Carol met Doug Clark and took him home with her. Carol listened to Doug's story of a mean landlady who had it out for him. The landlady was, in actuality, a girlfriend of Doug's, and their relationship was on the decline as well.

Needing to find accommodations, Doug had chosen Carol because she seemed sympathetic and easy to manipulate. He infrequently shared a bedroom with her and openly discussed his sexual escapades with other women; on a few occasions, he had even asked Carol to take photos of these happenings. Carol was having a difficult time making herself believe Doug wanted a relationship with her. Her fragile psyche would not allow her to believe that Jack and Doug were both merely using her.

Jeanette no longer saw Carol as any threat to her marriage to Jack. Carol, however, was still upset about Jack swindling money from her. When Carol confronted Jack about his deception, she was told he had used the money to pay off the loan on his van, and the remainder was used to refurbish and reupholster the van's interior. Jack took immense pride in the vehicle and used it as a rolling fortress of fornication.

A fake handicapped placard placed on the front dash insured Jack a convenient parking space and privacy while he carried on with prostitutes, exotic dancers, and other women in his life. Outfitted with carpet-covered benches and a crude area to wash up, it was the perfect spot for the quickies Jack enjoyed.

Carol had committed carnal acts with Jack inside the van and had seen, much to her chagrin, what she defined as "sleazy" women departing from the van and Jack's company after his set at Little Nashville. Jack had a voracious appetite for sex and kept a supply of porn he had made with his partners, sex toys, and bondage gear in his van. Carol, who seemed to only find value in herself if she were being made to feel desired and used as a sex object, was both enraged and hurt when Jack seemed to have lost interest in her as a sex partner.

She tried the same tactic she would use when Doug Clark was no longer interested in her sexually—bringing in another female. Jack told her in no uncertain terms that he would not have sex with her unless it was a ménage a trois, and Carol did her best to comply. Part of the problem was that most women, even those who were paid for their services, found Carol as distasteful a sexual partner as most men did.

Carol had happened on a solution. While moving three miles away from Valerio Gardens to an apartment which Jack had found for her on Lemona Avenue, she met an eleven-year-old girl—identified only in court documents by her first name to protect the identity of the underage child—named Shannon who impressed Carol by firing off a round of wisecracks and dirty jokes. Around Shannon, Carol would drift between the roles of an adult and as a peer of Shannon's own age. This ability allowed her to manipulate the young child in a very effective manner.

Carol, always desperate for a reason to talk to Jack, sought him out one night at Little Nashville, saying she was in trouble and needed to talk to him right away. Stifling his annoyance by reminding himself he could probably count on Carol to fork over some cash if he played his cards right, he agreed to meet her. When they met up, Carol wasted no time, according to a statement she later gave police, in detailing the murders Doug Clark had committed.

Jack listened as he sipped his drink, but the more Carol said, the harder it was for him to keep a straight face. She told him she knew too much and had seen too much. She described the "kill bag" Doug Clark carried in the car to commit murder. When she realized Jack was not taking her seriously, she pulled him over to the trunk of the car and showed him the proof.

This was serious; Jack told her and said that he needed to give this information to the police. It was then that Carol decided Jack had to die. She had told him too much.

Jack went back inside, and Carol followed a short time later. She slipped him a note, stating that if he agreed to have sex with her, she would set it up so he could have sex with Shannon. Carol knew the offer of pedophilic sex would be too strong for Jack to resist.

Jack told her to meet him at his van later. As the night wore on, Carol sipped her Sprite and kept an eye on Jack. She finally exited the club, making her way to her car with the intention of waiting for Jack, in case he tried to give her the slip as he had done on previous occasions.

She was angered to see Jack leave Little Nashville with another woman. This woman was involved in a sexual relationship with Jack Murray, Doug Clark, and Jack Murray's brother-in-law. It was from her that police would learn Carol was the last person seen with Jack.

The two entered Jack's van, and Carol waited as long as she could manage before going over and knocking on the side of the van. Neither of them seemed upset to see Carol, so she was uncertain whether she had interrupted anything. She hoped she had. Avril Roy-Smith told police she gave Carol a quick once over, told Jack goodnight, made her way back into Little Nashville, and spent the next few hours drinking with friends. Carol took her place in the van with the intention of discussing her concerns about Doug further.

Jack was not interested in talking and told Carol that as soon as she entered the van. Making his way to the back and the bench seats, Jack pulled down his pants around his ankles, and Carol was amused to see he was wearing some of his favorite undergarments—pink, lacy panties—the same kind worn by some of the Sunset Strip victims.

Positioning himself on his stomach, he said, "You know what I like." His abruptness made Carol angrier. When he asked her if she really intended to let him have the eleven-year-old, the only topic he did want to discuss, was the last straw.

Carol positioned herself behind Jack and used her hands to massage his penis before pressing her face in between his butt cheeks. Jack moaned, telling Carol how good that felt. Once again, however, he brought up Shannon, and as Carol continued the oral stimulation, she pressed the Raven handgun to the back of his head and pulled the trigger.

Jack's head slammed forward with the momentum of the bullet, and his anus clamped tightly on Carol's tongue. Now instead of moans, Jack was making a gurgling sound. Carol pumped another bullet into his skull, but Jack continued to make wet bubbling noises as he struggled to breathe.

Easing her hand into the waistband of her slacks, Carol pulled out a knife and stabbed Jack in the back nine times. While she stabbed him, she cursed him and called him names. She was not good enough for him; he would rather have a little girl. Well, she would give him what he deserved.

Carol checked Jack's pulse and was relieved to note he had finally succumbed to his injuries, but she was not finished yet. Still feeling frenzied, angry, and full of adrenaline, she stabbed and slashed his buttocks saying that he always wanted a piece of ass from someone, well she was going to take a piece of his ass. Jack was also known for enjoying forcing women to submit to sodomy and then cleaning his penis off with their mouth, so Carol ran the knife into his rectum over and over, asking him how he liked having something shoved up his ass.

By the time she had finished with him, Carol had realized that she was shaking. Breathing deeply, she planned her next move. She went over to the sink in the van, rinsed her hands, and then went to her car to retrieve the kill bag. Cleaning up as best she could, Carol happened to think that the bullets, which were lodged in Jack's brain, might be traced to her gun. As she saw it, she only had one option—get rid of the evidence.

Picking up the knife once more, Carol took hold of Jack's hair and shoved the knife into the back of his neck, prying apart the spinal column. With a sawing motion, Carol was finally able to remove Jack's head, which she then dropped in a plastic grocery bag and carried it to her car, placing it on the passenger seat.

Carol called the apartment where Doug and a girlfriend were spending the night shortly after three in the morning. She was laughing hysterically and not making a lot of sense as she tried to tell Doug what she had just done and that it was to protect him because Jack was going to go to the cops. Doug told Carol to shut up and get over to the apartment as quickly as possible.

When she arrived, an ambulance was at the apartment. Doug's girlfriend had suffered a seizure. Ever helpful, Carol asked the medics if she could be of any assistance since she was a nurse. The medics took one look at the crazed-looking woman and told her they had things under control.

Doug agreed to help Carol dispose of Jack's head, and they both got in the car, Carol saying they should find a fence post and leave Jack's head to be found by some poor unsuspecting soul—that would be a real gas, she giggled. Doug pulled up to a trashcan and told Carol to chuck the head in it. Disappointed at this anticlimactic end to her adventure, she did as she was told.

Four days later, the police received a call about a van parked on a street that seemed to be emitting a horribly foul odor. Upon arriving at the scene, the police recognized the smell of decomposition, a smell that, once experienced, can never be forgotten. Detectives arrived to inspect the scene and noticed an expended bullet casing. It would prove to be more important than they could have ever imagined.

It would not be long before Carol would tell startled co-workers about murdering Jack and participating in the Sunset Strip murders. Police would receive a phone call from them as well as from Carol herself claiming to have been working in conjunction with her lover to kill the women.

She went to her apartment to begin gathering evidence the officers would need to put both herself and her lover away for a long time—perhaps forever.

IV

Dastardly Doug

THE "KING OF ONE NIGHT STANDS." THAT WAS how Doug Clark preferred to think of himself. Standing at six feet tall with thinning, straggly blond hair, and somewhat beady hooded eyes, it is not immediately evident what physical traits drew women to him.

Perhaps knowing this, he concentrated his efforts on learning how to woo women with his words and then tempted them with the depravity that truly made up Douglas Daniel Clark.

Like the proverbial spider bidding its potential prey, the fly, into its parlor, Clark learned what women wanted to hear and fed them those sugar-coated lies until they were firmly entangled in his web of deception and perversion.

Born in 1948 to Franklyn, a naval officer, and Blanch, a homemaker, Douglas Daniel Clark grew up the third youngest of his four siblings, all of whom agree that their parents doted on Doug. His brother, Walter, theorizes that the reason Franklyn and Blanch thought his brother was so perfect was that he was a con artist and pathological liar.

A heavy dose of denial and a belief in Doug's lies seemed to be their parents' way of dealing with unsavory situations. Franklyn's position in the military, and the resultant work experience involved, offered him the opportunity to travel and work all over the world. Blanch and the Clark children traveled with him.

Doug never had any interest in academics, and his school records reflected that fact. It would be later in life that he learned he had the ability to impress women by having a small amount of knowledge on various topics. One line of Shakespeare here, a few statistics quoted there, and anyone speaking only briefly with Doug was left with the impression he was educated. That was all part of his heavily crafted façade.

Doug's early life is a bit of a mystery, and that's the way he intends to keep it. The little that is known is mostly what Doug himself has attested to in interviews and during testimony at trial. His parents were called to testify during his trial for multiple murders, but they chose the selective memory route, often denying circumstances and anything they testified to which Doug disagreed with, he dismissed or formally objected to.

As a teenager, Doug developed a taste for both alcohol and older women. Older, overweight women to be more precise. Girls his own age showed little interest in the awkward teen, especially after word got around that any girl who was intimate with Doug ran the risk of having the act documented on film, and the photographs passed out among classmates.

Soon, Doug came to realize the opportunities available to him by sharing the pleasure of his company with lonely women. Ironically, or perhaps not so ironically, if one values the teachings of Freud, almost all the women Doug would become involved with throughout his life resembled his mother, Blanch. The sexual experiences offered by these women were invaluable to Doug, as was the psychology he learned from them, which he would use in his relationships.

After graduation, Doug was drafted into the military. He chose the Air Force and trained in radio intelligence—a strategic move by Doug to keep himself away from the front lines in Vietnam. Like Jack Murray, Doug would tell people impressive, but impossible, stories of hand-to-hand combat and being a prisoner of war. Attention at any cost was something both men and their lover, Carol Bundy, chased tirelessly.

In 1976, Doug married a woman three years his senior he had met in a North Hollywood bar. Beverly, like so many of the women Doug was involved with, was older, blond, overweight. Doug and Beverly opened an upholstery business that never really got off the ground. According to both Doug and Beverly, there was genuine affection between the two, but Doug could not or would not remain monogamous and, although Doug showed promise and talent with any work he undertook, he lacked the drive to become a success.

The couple divorced after four years but remained lifelong friends, with Beverly even testifying at Doug's murder trial. It was Doug's failure to try to make something of himself that caused Beverly to give up on the relationship and had nothing to do with the fact that Doug wore women's underwear, she told the court emphatically. She also stated that that aspect of Doug's life had never bothered her, and she thought no more about his affinity for wearing panties than his interest in wife swapping or threesomes.

Doug bounced from one menial job to another with no real ambition for most of the 1970s. While they were married, Beverly had suggested Doug apply for a position that had opened up with the city for a steam plant trainee. Doug applied for and got the job. This training and work experience led to the last job he would have in the outside world.

Doug was making decent money as a boiler operator at the local Jergens plant in 1980. Whether he had been spending too much money on hookers and strippers or just mismanaged his pay, by early 1980, he was getting desperate for cash. He was still running his usual scams in which he made the rounds to bars and sought out the loneliest woman in the room. He would soon ingratiate himself to his new acquaintance before plying her with a sob story about his wicked landlady who was kicking him out.

Doug had no scruples about using women for sex, a place to stay, or anything else he could manage to get out of them. Usually, the woman would offer him a spot on her couch to crash on, if not her bed. By his account, Doug said these women knew he was using them and that these relationships were nonexclusive. Whatever the case, shortly after Christmas 1979, Carol Bundy met Doug and immediately moved him into her apartment.

It happened when Carol found herself once again at Little Nashville sipping a drink and pining away for her sometime lover Jack Murray, who sang Tom Jones cover tunes. Jack was doing his best to pretend Carol Bundy did not exist, so when Carol locked eyes with a gentleman she had never seen before, one who actually maintained eye contact instead of looking away the way most people did when they saw Carol, she was intrigued.

Doug, correctly judging Carol to be an easy mark, introduced himself and asked her to dance. They went back to Carol's place that night, and when Doug talked and played easily with her two sons, she thought she had won the lottery. When it was time to put the boys to bed, they asked if Doug would come in to say goodnight.

Doug moved in with Carol right away but established his own space with a small cot. If Doug couldn't find action anywhere else, he might sleep in Carol's bed with her. What happened with greater frequency as time passed was Doug asking Carol to sleep on the cot or the living room couch because he had brought another woman home, and as he told the judge at his murder trial—the activities required a queen-size bed.

Doug never kept his conquests a secret, and in fact, he moved in and out of Carol's apartment whenever he was seeing a new woman. The few that he brought around Carol did not question the living arrangements, but they certainly did not feel comfortable or welcome.

The intimate relationship he and Carol had shared was a thing of the past. Now he referred to her as "Steppin Fetchitt," meaning that she was little more than a servant who would attend to his basic needs: food and laundry.

V
Big City, Little Rock

Duringhis own sentencing hearing a decade and a half after the Sunset Strip murders, convicted serial killer Joel Rifkin addressed the notion that if he were locked away from society, citizens would heave a collective sigh of relief and sleep soundly at night. This was a false feeling of security, Rifkin told the court. On any given day, Rifkin said, there are other serial killers "walking the streets right now."

Law enforcement was well aware of this, as they focused on nabbing the killer responsible for the Sunset Strip murders. Police feared the public might grow hysterical as they had during the

Manson Family and Ted Bundy murders. Citizens on edge buy guns they are not equipped to handle safely.

While many Californians were listening to news of the killings with a sense of dread, it was a sense of curiosity that led to a grisly discovery. If he were able to turn back time and reverse the choice that he had made that June day in 1980, then Jonathan Caravello would not have chosen to open and gaze into the wooden box he found occupying the parking space he normally used. But like the fabled box belonging to Pandora, Caravello was unable to stifle his curiosity and had to know what mysteries the box contained. Once opened, the box unleashed a nightmare not easily forgotten, and a mystery not easily solved.

California, Hollywood in particular, has long been a place in which people envision their dreams coming true. Ever since the first movie studio opened in the Los Angeles area in 1911, people have descended in droves with dreams of celebrity and stardust in their eyes. The movies fill us with a sense of magic and wonder, but the seedy area surrounding these dream factories, especially at night, is a place of nightmares. Ask any beat cop or homicide detective, and they will tell you a harsh dose of reality is quickly injected straight into the bloodstream of most girls arriving in the big city with their big dreams.

Hardcore reality and the need to survive blur the lines of one's personal moral codes, as it courses through their veins. It is a reality full of hunger and desperation, often leading to syringes filled with heroin to skew and muffle that reality. Where there are desperation and substance abuse, the "world's oldest profession" can also be found being employed to feed those addictions and temporarily snuff out feelings of desperation that creep in, dragging jagged claws across memories of a time before life on the street.

Most little girls do not grow up dreaming of being a $30 call girl, walking the track night after night, dodging cops, hoarding money to escape from violent pimps. Serial killers from "Jack the Ripper" to the "Green River Killer" have known that prostitutes, by the very nature of their profession, are often easy victims. It is not unusual for bodies to turn up in the county morgues that go unidentified and unclaimed. Even families actively looking for a missing loved one must often resolve themselves to the fact they might never know what happened to a missing girl once she has been out working the streets.

Exie LaFaye Wilson was only twenty years old at the time of her death. Long and lean, with an almost cadaverous appearance even in life, mug shots and postmortem photos show a woman who appears to be twice that age. Weary of the life she was leading, Exie had told her mother she was done with hooking. Street life had aged her well beyond her years, and the strain was becoming too much to bear.

Exie had been raised in a small town near Little Rock, Arkansas, by her mother, Velma, a widow. When Exie's father had passed away, Velma struggled to raise her daughters, but most of Exie's zest for life seemed to have died when her father did. Barely literate, she managed to graduate high school but was discouraged by the lack of prospects her poor education offered her.

Exie had waitressed and worked as a hotel maid for a short time before meeting and falling in love with Derrick Albright, a pimp from Little Rock. Whether she wanted to turn tricks to make money that turned out to be only slightly better than what she had made at her previous jobs, or simply did it out of love as her sister believes, Exie began working for Albright and was soon arrested for solicitation.

On June 12, 1980, the same day Gina Marano and her stepsister, Cynthia Chandler, were murdered, she called her mother four separate times, telling her she was leaving Albright for good and coming home. She was not only tired of the lifestyle, but she was also tired of being arrested. Besides, she said, the Little Rock cops were doing such a good job making arrests that customers were wary. Business had gotten so bad that her boyfriend, Albright, wanted to travel to California and try plying their trade there. Exie had no desire to continue working as a prostitute, especially traveling so far away from her mother.

During the last phone call, Albright grabbed the phone from Exie and told Zelma to leave them alone and stay out of their business. It had been a month since Zelma had seen her daughter, and she had no idea as she told her daughter goodbye at the end of that last phone call in June that the next time that she saw her daughter, it would be to plan her funeral.

Exie was not the only woman in Albright's life. The group he was taking with him to Los Angeles, where his parents lived, consisted of four other women. There was Willie, two different women who both went by the name Sharon, and Karen Jones. Exie was friendly with the other girls, but she was not interested in forging particularly strong friendships with any of them, although Karen Jones was sort of an exception.

Physically, the two women were polar opposites, with Exie being a skinny-as-a-rail bleached blonde and Karen being a heavyset brunette. Part of the excess weight belonging to Karen was due to the baby she was carrying. The baby was the reason Karen had turned to prostitution. She was desperate to be able to support herself and her unborn child.

Karen had been attending college on a scholarship when she learned of the pregnancy. Unable to continue her education at that time, and unsure of where to go for assistance, she had stayed at a battered women's shelter before meeting Albright. She did not want to sell her body, but she thought of it as a necessary evil and a temporary solution until her son was born.

The group made it from Arkansas to California in four days, and the girls were eager to see the sights and start making money. The first couple of days were devoted to sightseeing and scoping out the territory and competition. On Friday, the girls went on a mini shopping spree, and Exie bought herself a brand-new pink dress, which she planned on wearing the following night to look for customers.

Saturday night, the girls headed out to find work while Albright shot pool and sipped drinks. At one point, Karen reached Albright on the phone to let him know a police officer had given her a warning and told her to move along. She was going to do just that and told Albright she would be working up the Strip closer to the city limits.

Around the same time that Karen was talking on the phone to Albright, the girls said they saw Exie walking alone on the other side of the Sunset Strip looking for a date. That was the last time any of them ever saw or spoke to Exie Wilson and Karen Jones.

Darkness made it difficult for the police officer to tell what had happened to the woman lying on the pavement. At first, he thought perhaps she had been walking along the side of the road and had been the victim of a hit and run. Hit and runs were not very common in this area, but with the number of streetwalkers who frequented dark, poorly lit environments, it was a possibility. It could just as likely have been the result of an argument with a pimp or John who ran the girl down in the heat of the moment.

Kneeling down next to the girl's prone figure, it was difficult to tell much about her looks. Her hair stuck in strings to the blood covering her face. Someone's daughter; this was someone's daughter lying here. The officer had no idea that had she lived, Karen would also have been someone's mother.

Just a few short hours later, and only a short distance away, someone discovered a woman's nude body lying near a dumpster in the parking lot of a restaurant. Even more shocking and startling than the fact that the woman's body was missing all its clothing, was that it was also missing its head.

The amount of blood at the scene was staggering. Doug would bring up a point during the trial that the amount of blood at the Jack Murray homicide was minute compared to the Exie Wilson crime scene. Doug speculated this was because Carol and/or Jack had cut off Exie's head while she was unconscious, but still alive. Because her heart was still beating when she was decapitated, the amount of blood was vast. With the Jack Murray decapitation, Carol used what she had learned with the Exie Wilson murder and waited until she was certain Jack was dead before decapitating him. This kept the amount of blood spillage minimal compared to Exie's.

The reason for removing a victim's head is to make identifying them more difficult. With no head, no clothing, or identification, police knew the task would not be an easy one.

The police had no idea at the time that the woman's head would not be discovered for days. The circumstances surrounding the discovery were odd and obviously meant to be shocking. When Jonathan Caravello returned from his job in the wee hours before sunrise, he spotted an object in the parking space he normally used.

Curious, he exited the vehicle and discovered what at first appeared to be a small, wooden treasure chest.

Hoping he had come across something of great value, Jonathan was a little disheartened to note the box had been broken when it made contact with the pavement. Now he was not so sure there would be anything salvageable if the contents were also damaged. At first, it just appeared to be clothing someone had stored in the box and discarded, but pulling aside the layers of fabric, Caravello was horrified and sickened to find the head of a young woman. Gasping and dropping the girl's head, Caravello fled to call the police.

VI
Melancholic Marnette

LONG BEFORE THE TELEVISION SHOW 77 SUNSET Strip found its way into American homes in the 1950s and 1960s, even before Gloria Swanson's character in the film Sunset Boulevard stated she was ready for her close up, the mile and a half stretch of land had a reputation for seediness and lawlessness.

Detectives on the aforementioned television show were capable of nabbing a criminal and tidying up all loose ends in under an hour, until the next episode, but real-life justice was not usually nearly that swift. The area that is known as Sunset Boulevard, or the "Sunset Strip," has as many names as the deadly duo who were to become associated with it.

The year 1980 found headlines in Los Angeles touting graphic crimes by someone the news and television referred to as the "Sunset Slasher," or the "Sunset Slayer," as well as the "Sunset Murderer," along with other variations. The killer was so dubbed because the murder victims were young women known to frequent the "strip," most of whom were prostitutes.

Murder, Prostitution, Vice—none of these things were new to the strip. It is easy to see, even today, by looking into the eyes of women who still work the area, that the strip, with its drug use and physical violence that are the norm there, has *stripped them*—of their souls and often their very will to live.

Sunset Boulevard runs from Hollywood through to Beverly Hills and is intersected by streets which house famous clubs and music venues such as the Whisky-a-GoGo where Jim Morrison of The Doors drank, drugged, and performed his unique style of haunting melodies, and the Viper Room which saw the death of River Phoenix by drug overdose in 1993.

Drugs and alcohol have always been readily available around the strip, going all the way back to the 1920s and Prohibition. Gangsters and speakeasies were the special of the day, and gambling, sex, or anything else a person was looking for was always available if the price was right. One of the things gangsters and other people working to the left side of the law were aware and took advantage of was the fact that the area fell outside the jurisdiction of the Los Angeles Police Department and the laws which applied to the city itself.

Sunset Strip was a virtual land unto itself, and in many ways, it still is. The glitz and glamour associated with it was merely a façade. By early 1980, when a killer was stalking them, the prostitutes did not bear any resemblance to tarnished angels or fallen doves, as they were called in a bygone era, as much as they resembled desperation and hopelessness.

Among the sea of broken bottles and broken people, a seventeen-year-old girl stood, wishing for a breeze to provide relief that never came. Her naturally curly blond hair was thick and the heat, even this late at night, made her wish she had chosen to wear her hair pulled up. Wearing her hair down gave her the appearance of being older, which had a two-fold effect. One, it kept the Pedo Pervs who were looking for young girls at a distance, and two, it kept the police from hassling her about being a runaway.

Marnette Comer looked every bit the same age as her nineteen-year-old sister Sabra. Marnette's girl-next-door beauty was the epitome of the California babes that The Beach Boys had sung about. Far from wholesome, however, Marnette's existence much more closely resembled that of the girls Motley Crue would sing about occupying the Sunset Strip years after Marnette had been laid to rest.

The second oldest of five children, Marnette Carrie Comer was born in Sacramento, California, on May 21, 1963, to Ellen and Gerald Comer. Marnette, like her older sister, was a prostitute who worked the nightshift along Sunset Boulevard. Marnette had started selling her body as soon as she became a teenager and ran away from home repeatedly, finally landing in a girls' home for juvenile delinquents.

In January 1980, Marnette's mother picked her up from the girls' home for a dentist appointment and planned to take her daughter shopping afterward. The two never got to do any shopping. While waiting in an exam room in the dental office, Marnette took the opportunity while alone to climb out of the window. Her mother never saw her again.

Marnette's younger sister answered the phone when she called a month prior to her disappearance and had begged her older sister to come home, but Marnette refused. Sabra also worried about her little sister, but Marnette assured her that she usually worked in tandem with another prostitute or took her customers back to a room. In her mind, this was safer than getting into a car alone and letting the john decide where he would take her and what he would do with her. Plus, Marnette added with her usual mirthfulness, she could fight like a wildcat if needed.

As Marnette stood on the sidewalk talking to Sabra, her eyes scanned her surroundings. Someone lay in the gutter, dead or close to it. Her nose was assaulted by the smell of garbage—both human garbage and the refuse they created. The noise of unhappy people co-existing made her ears ring. Sirens screamed. Hookers screamed. Pimps screamed.

She was done. She was going to stop hooking. Maybe she would move back home and look into getting her GED. Sabra noted her sister's grim look of determination, which contrasted so starkly with the pink t-shirt she was wearing that read "Daddy's Girl." Their biological father had not been much of a "daddy." The sentiment applied more to the pimp who took almost every cent they brought in, who feared that if a girl had money that she might leave him, just as Marnette said she was planning.

No one saw the john who picked Marnette up that night, and no one saw her again until two people, hiking through the hills above the city, stumbled upon a filthy, old mattress. Protruding from underneath were the leathery remains of a person, but they could not be sure because of the state of the body, whether it was male or female. Left outside, and exposed to the elements, the body had become mummified.

The murder weapon was determined to be just like the one used to murder the prior suspected victims of the "Sunset Strip Killer." Judging by the state of the body, it was ascertained this victim had probably been killed before the Marano-Chandler murders, which police had taken to be the first deaths. Marnette Comer's killer had not only shot her but had also gutted her with a sharp knife, and it appeared a crude attempt at organ removal had occurred.

It is possible that the partial disembowelment was not done to satisfy the killer's bloodlust but as an effort to speed up decomposition. Exposure to weather and wildlife provides a better explanation than a killer attempting to retrieve organs. If someone were that intent on removing body parts, surely this secluded location would have been the perfect spot for such endeavors. This was not "Jack the Ripper" removing body parts on a busy London sidewalk. A killer could take their time and leisurely slice away.

Police knew who their victim was, and the type of weapon and ammunition used, but they were still a long way off from finding the killer. The crazy thing is, after the discovery of Exie Wilson and Karen Jones, the police knew the same weapon had been used for all of the murders. Pulling a list of .25 caliber Ravens sold in the area, the police learned only thirty of those guns had been sold that year and two Raven handguns, identical except for one being nickel-plated while the other was plated in silver, had been purchased by a woman named Carol Bundy. Police weren't looking for a woman, though.

Police had Carol's phone and license plate number, address, and driver's license information from the permit she was required to fill out in order to purchase the guns. Had they followed up on this information, they would have possibly realized by merely talking to her that her voice matched the voice captured on the recording of the woman calling herself Betsy/Claudia; the phone call police received right after the Marano-Chandler murders. It is also possible that, given Carol's fragile mental state, she might have cracked and admitted to everything right then, thereby sparing a few lives.

Marnette's death, like those of the other victims, was nothing she brought upon herself, regardless of the circumstances of her personal life. Yes, she lived a high-risk lifestyle, but that does not give anyone the right to take another person's life. Police are sworn to serve and protect, but in many instances during this investigation, they missed their mark merely by their narrow-minded approach.

More than once, the police would admit, inadvertently, that information had pointed them in the direction of Carol Bundy. Even though they were not "looking for a woman" while searching for the killer(s), however; had they taken a moment to talk to Carol and those who knew her, it would have soon become apparent she was "either the killer or someone who knows the killer," just like the label on the tape recording attested. Carol would have led them to either Doug or Jack.

If only they had been more open-minded and willing to consider a female as their main suspect.

VII
A Short Story About Shannon

BY THE AGE OF ELEVEN, SHANNON HAD ALREADY learned to distrust adults and authority figures and harbored a growing resentment against her mother. Repeatedly molested by a friend of the family, she knew the abuse was not her mother's fault, because she had not told her mother—or anyone else for that matter. The heavy petting and touching were something she had grown to believe that were acts that adults performed on children and were to be tolerated and kept secret.

When the girl first saw Carol Bundy moving into an empty apartment in her complex, she did not pay much attention. Carol was the type of person easily overlooked by everyone. When she overheard the plump woman in the huge glasses cursing as she strained to move things into her new place, Shannon fired off a string of curse words herself. They exchanged off-color jokes, and both laughed, taking an instant liking to one another.

Shannon's mother was almost young enough to be Carol's daughter. She was, by her own admission as well as Shannon's account, busy with her own life, and not very involved in her young daughter's. Carol was nothing like the slow-witted woman she appeared to be, and Shannon loved it.

Shannon's mother, Jacqueline, was, at first, skeptical about letting her daughter spend so much time with Carol, but upon meeting her, and witnessing how much happier her daughter seemed since making a new friend, she pushed her worries aside. Carol and Shannon developed a close relationship and spent time shopping, cooking, and watching television.

Shannon was soon keeping secrets about her new friend from her mother, just as she had with the other adults who touched her and played games with her. Shannon admitted later that, at first, she was not sure how she felt about the sexual relationship that had developed, but she was certain that had she ever wanted to stop or discontinue things, Carol would never have forced her to do anything.

Shannon was introduced to not only lesbian sex acts, but also when Carol and Doug became involved, Shannon was incorporated into their sex life as well. Shannon says she enjoyed wearing the lingerie her two friends bought for her, having her makeup and hair done by Carol for the Polaroid pictures the older woman took of her and Doug.

She might not have understood the full implication of what she and Doug were doing in the photos or what it would mean if they were ever discovered, but she did understand that Doug seemed disappointed they only pretended to do the things captured in the pictures. In one, Doug was dressed in not much more than a dog collar with a leash and Shannon was wearing lingerie, her stiletto heel grinding into Doug's neck as he bowed in a submissive pose. Doug wanted Shannon to paddle him, but she refused. It was all too silly.

The three would participate in mutual oral sex acts, but Shannon drew the line at allowing Doug to have vaginal sex with her. The technical terms weren't something she was familiar with, but she had a rough understanding of what virginity was, and she wanted to keep hers. Carol convinced Shannon to take some medicine one night that would relax her and make her drowsy so that Doug could attempt sex with the girl. At first compliant, as Doug began and the experience became painful, Shannon screamed out and told him to stop, which he did.

Carol also introduced Shannon to Jack Murray, who was instantly smitten with the child and begged Carol to let him have her as a gift. Shannon had not minded spending time with Doug Clark because if anything, he was nervous and almost intimidated around her. If she said she wanted to eat at a certain restaurant, he took her there, and just to test the hold she had over him, Shannon would say that she had changed her mind, and they would proceed to a different eatery.

Doug constantly gave her gifts and took her places. He was almost like a puppy dog, so eager to please. That was what had struck Shannon as being so funny when he had worn the dog collar and leash in photos—it had been perfectly ironic. Doug insisted Shannon choose the pornography he enjoyed perusing as well as the prostitutes he picked up.

Doug and Shannon would cruise down the Sunset Strip, Doug asking Shannon's opinion on the streetwalkers they passed.

Shannon was quick to rule out any that she termed "ugly" and enjoyed the power of making such adult decisions. Once, the pair happened upon a prostitute with a particularly large bosom, and as she climbed into the car, Doug whispered to Shannon to say something racy.

The hooker had barely recognized Shannon's presence until Shannon spoke up and said, "Nice jugs, babe." The hooker exited the car as quickly as possible, no doubt realizing that although she might have seen a lot while working the track, she did not understand the dynamics of the duo who had just picked her up. Doug and Shannon laughed about the incident.

With Jack Murray, however, Shannon did not feel comfortable. There was something ominous and threatening about the man. Frankly, he gave her the creeps. That was saying a lot. Carol was told, in the nicest way possible, that there was no way in hell Shannon ever wanted to be in Jack's presence again.

Carol, confused as usual, began to have guilty feelings about the sexual relationship she was carrying on with Shannon. Taking Shannon with her, Carol went to discuss things with a family therapist. The therapist questioned Shannon in regard to her feelings about the sexual acts she had taken part in. Hearing

Shannon say that she did not really mind having sex with the two adults and appearing very well-grounded and emotionally healthy, the therapist stated it was not his job to moralize the situation and left the decision whether or not to continue being sexually involved with Doug and Carol up to Shannon.

Shannon would receive a card from Doug a decade after he was first incarcerated, wishing her a happy birthday. The content quickly turned grim as he detailed how he had planned to murder Shannon on her twelfth birthday. Doug is one of those people who revels in the ability to manipulate people's feelings. A few of the people who have interviewed Doug during his incarceration have said they got the impression he was trying to manipulate them, their feelings, and opinions regarding him and his role in the murders the entire time they were with him.

As Shannon has suggested, and it is quite obvious that Doug Clark has manipulated the press into writing about his version of Shannon at age eleven. He describes the events in a way that seems to place blame on the victim as if she were a "Mini Mata Hari," as Shannon puts it. Doug Clark will never take responsibility for his own actions regarding Shannon. It was Carol's fault… It was Shannon's fault… But never his own.

Shannon has said that Carol became aware of Doug's intention to kill her on her twelfth birthday and by turning him in as the "Sunset Strip Killer," Doug's plans were thwarted, thereby saving Shannon's life. Although it might be due to Carol's actions that Shannon is alive and Doug is behind bars, it is difficult to call any action of Carol's heroic. If anything, it seems she is even more culpable for the crimes committed against Shannon because it was she who introduced Shannon to Doug, and it was also she who knew that the relationship she was entering into with a child of eleven was vastly inappropriate.

Doug had gifted Shannon with clothing and a music box keychain that played music. Shannon had noticed that the keychain, which played the classic *Greensleeves*, was scratched up and had definitely not been bought brand new from a store. The clothing, inappropriate for a young girl and clearly intended for older females, was also obviously pre-owned.

Only after police arrested Doug and came to talk with Shannon and take possession of these items did she begin to wonder if these objects had belonged to Doug's victims. Even more unsettling to ponder, were these objects which had belonged to prostitutes she had personally selected for Doug on the excursions the two had taken in search of prostitutes? Had he gone back at a later time without Shannon present and killed these women, then gifted their belongings to her?

It is a thought which is almost unfathomable in its depravity.

VIII

Confession Time

A CALL CAME INTO THE LOS ANGELES POLICE department on June 14, 1980, from a person claiming to have information regarding the murders of Gina Marano and Cynthia Chandler. An officer took the call and spoke directly with the female caller, who would not identify herself to police, but instead, gave her name as Betsy, while a second officer listened in on an extension. The woman was only on the line long enough to give the false name and purpose for the call before it was suddenly disconnected. The only option for police was to wait and hope that Betsy—whomever she actually was—would call back.

Two hours later, she did exactly that, explaining she had made the initial call from a payphone and panicked when a police officer passed by. She had hung up, not certain whether to call back. Police were glad she had decided to make a second phone call and had taken time to ensure the conversation would be recorded in the event she called again.

As the tape began recording the conversation, the woman explained her reason for contacting them. The reason for her nervousness and hesitation, she said, was her fear of the killer. She told the officer that she felt that her life was in danger simply by speaking with them. Betsy also indicated, as already suspected, she was using a pseudonym.

Upon thinking this over, she decided the name Betsy was not safe to use because the person that she feared was the murderer would associate that name with her. Make it Claudia, she told the officer, before changing her mind once again and saying both names could be attributed to her by the killer—who she made certain to mention was also her live-in lover. Forget both names, she told the cop. If she felt comfortable, then she would reveal her true name in a day or two. Just forget the Betsy/Claudia business, or else she was going to end up just like those girls.

To what girls were she referring to, the officer inquired? The two dead girls that were just found up off the Ventura Freeway was the reply. Her friend, actually her lover, she quickly amended, had shown up at her apartment covered in blood and confessed he had murdered them and had had sex with their corpses before dumping them where they had, at last, been found.

Clearly, the officer thought, the individual on the line seemed nervous and anxious, but she also seemed unstable. Not just the temporary sort of mental instability found in a passing moment of fear either. A passing moment of fear is when you are startled by seeing your image unexpectedly reflected by a mirror in a darkened room. But the level of crazy displayed by the caller was the kind that, just when you think you have reached the bottom, there is a whole sub-basement level of crazy waiting for you.

Pushing aside all the mental health issues and visions of rubber-walled rooms the caller had either spent time in or should be currently occupying, the police focused on the information being given that was actually applicable to the case.

Carol Bundy huddled over the payphone and cradled the telephone receiver close to her mouth, pushed her thick-lensed glasses up on her nose, and took a deep breath. She wanted to check some facts her lover had told her about the murders, she said. Police informed her they would not give out any information on an active investigation, nor would they confirm any information she supplied them.

Nervously licking her lips and taking a deep breath, Carol said she understood. The officer told Carol she was welcome to share anything she felt might aid the investigation, but the police would not be participating in the share and tell.

"All right," Carol told them, she just needed a minute to think things through.

"Take your time," the officer assured her.

Carol was extremely evasive when answering the police officers' questions. Asked if the man she thought was the killer was black or white, Carol responded, "Yes."

"Which one?" the officers asked.

"Either one—both," she answered.

She wanted to know if it was true that both girls had been shot, and the police told her that information had appeared in the newspaper. In order to be taken seriously, she would need to provide information only the killer, or someone the killer confided in, would know. Not to be deterred, Carol agreed that that was true, but the papers had not stated where or how many times the girls had been shot.

They were not there to answer her questions; they were running the investigation, not her, they reminded her. Carol made them promise the two aliases she had used would not appear in the paper. In a very matter-of-fact manner, the police informed her she had not shared anything with them that a paper would be remotely interested in printing. Eighty-five percent of what she was saying was misdirection, Carol said and asked if they understood. No, they replied, they did not understand any of this.

Carol went on to tell them her boyfriend was 41—the same age as Jack. She also claimed her boyfriend had told her that he had been committing murders since he was a teenager, and the total number of victims was around 50. She then told the police that her boyfriend had borrowed her car one night, and when she went to retrieve it, she found a bag containing white towels and a blanket covered in blood, along with some women's clothing.

She had gone directly to a laundromat, she said, and washed the bloodied items, before carefully wiping down the inside of the washing machine. A wad of blood-soaked paper towels had been disposed of in a trashcan. She refused to give a location where she had dumped the evidence.

Her boyfriend was extremely violent, Carol said, and she feared that not only had he killed these two girls, but she believed him when he told her these were not his first murders. The urge to kill was so strong for him that the only way to stop him was to lock him away.

The officers reminded Carol that so far, she had not provided them with any information strong enough to investigate the possibility that her boyfriend was the killer.

Before Carol was able to provide police officers with any evidence of value, the switchboard operator accidentally disconnected the phone call, much to officers' relief and disappointment. It had not been a very profitable or fruitful conversation. Despite their exasperation, the two police officers affixed a label to the tape, which had been used to record the phone call. The handwritten label read, "Either the killer or someone who knows the killer."

The suggestion which Doug would make—that Carol had decapitated both Exie Wilson and Jack Murray, is bolstered by the fact that Carol made phone calls to police after both murders. The murders, oddly enough, occurred at almost the same time of day. Upon examining both heads and the jagged skin flaps, which would have attached the heads to their respective necks, the medical examiner stated he believed both decapitations were committed by the same person.

IX

The Cuckoo Cracks

BY THE END OF JULY, CAROL WAS BARELY ABLE TO function. Her behavior at work, always strange, had gotten so erratic that her co-workers began actively avoiding her. Calling up her old friend Richard Geis, she told him that Doug was the serial killer that the police were looking for, and she felt that she was his next target because she knew too much. Get out, Geis advised her, just get the hell away from him.

She could not do that, she told her friend. Only she could stop Doug Clark from continuing to kill, and she had to find a way. Geis told her to be careful, and Carol thanked him before hanging up. She promptly called back and told him she had only been joking.

She stated she was writing a story, and merely wanted to test out the material on him. Geis thought she was lying but said nothing.

Instead of talking to Doug, she decided to leave him a note. It stated that she had decided to end her life because she could no longer live without Doug, or with the guilt she carried over the murders. She left the note in plain sight for Doug to find, went out to the garage and slid behind the wheel of her Datsun.

Waiting what she felt was a sufficient amount of time for Doug to find the note and come looking for her, she sighed, realizing she would now have to actually go through with her suicide plan. Carol pulled out the drugs she had brought with her. The romantic in Carol hoped that, at any moment, Doug would come running into the garage in tears, begging her not to do it.

Being a *diabetic*, Carol knew that an overdose of insulin was easy to accomplish and virtually pain-free—except for possible seizures and convulsions when the glucose levels drop suddenly. Being a *nurse*, Carol knew she could probably counter those potential side effects with Librium, of which she had a large supply.

Injecting herself with twelve hundred and fifty milligrams of insulin and one hundred milligrams of Librium, she then decided not to take any chances and rifled through her purse until she found the prescription bottle of Librium. Popping an additional one hundred milligrams of the drug in her mouth, she settled back into her seat and awaited the effects. The Librium soon made her extremely drowsy, and it was becoming difficult to think. What was she doing parked in the garage? Had she been going somewhere, or had she just returned?

Deciding in her drowsy stupor she must have been going somewhere, she started the engine and headed the car in the direction she normally went when commuting to work. She awoke to sirens and flashing lights—people she did not know surrounded her, talking in loud, anxious tones.

Carol had driven two blocks from her apartment to the parking lot of her favorite restaurant. In her drugged state, she had called the hospital where she worked to let them know she was killing herself, would be unable to work the next day, and hoped they could find another nurse to cover her shift. Confused as to what was occurring, Carol's supervisor at the hospital called the apartment and reached Doug Clark. He had never even read the suicide note Carol had left for him.

Carol was taken to the hospital for evaluation and observation. She was keenly aware that Doug had neither called to check on her condition nor come by to see her. When the staff told her she would be discharged, she called Jack Murray for a ride. Jack arrived with one of the dancers from Little Nashville, who he and Doug were sleeping with. Carol was aware that both men were sleeping with other women and not her, but this seemed to her as especially inconsiderate. She had planned to commit suicide because neither man wanted her, and Jack was picking her up with this tramp.

The three piled into Jack's van. It was decided they would stop for fast food on the way home. Carol, still miffed that Jack had brought someone else along, eyed the other woman and said she only wanted a Diet Coke. Jack and his lady friend sat up front laughing and eating, and Carol became incensed and decided she would rather walk home. She took her drink to go.

The failed suicide was not Carol's first, but as a nurse, and with her knowledge of medications, it seems this was once again a half-hearted attempt. She had access to both drugs as well as firearms. Carol related to police she had decided to end her life in June. Parked outside a Baskin-Robbins, Carol placed the barrel of the loaded gun in her mouth but could not find the courage to pull the trigger.

If Carol had truly wanted to die and life had become unbearable, then why did she report to both police and Jack that she was afraid Doug was going to kill her? Would that not bring about the end of her life, which she said she so desired but was unable to do herself?

After the discovery of Jack's body and the subsequent interviews by police, Carol was out of Librium and out of her mind. Unable to sleep and unable to keep going on as she had before Jack's murder, she went to work on August 11 and informed the head nurse she was walking out on the job.

She had called her friend Richard Geis that morning and begged him to give her a place to stay. Geis, in a matter-of-fact manner which he hoped would ensure that Carol did not misconstrue the message as she was often wont to do, told her it was impossible, and he had no desire to be with her ever again.

With this final rejection, Carol reconciled it was time to contact the police and turn herself in.

As Carol related to her supervisor that her boyfriend—Jack—had not been the victim of an accident, but had, in reality, been murdered, her co-worker was suddenly all ears. She then proceeded to tell him that her other boyfriend—Doug—had committed the

Sunset Strip murders. Her supervisor wasted no time in making sure the police were en route to the hospital.

The hospital was placed in lockdown as police arrived and swarmed the building. In something one would expect to take place in a scene from a comedic movie, Carol evaded the police by mere chance—she took an elevator down while police took the other elevator up to the floor the call had originated from.

It was just one of the many strange happenings in the story of Carol Bundy.

The next logical step, in Carol's mind at least, was to notify Doug at work of her confession to co-workers and imminent arrest by police. She urged him to take what money she had and get as far away as possible. When Doug heard that Carol, the woman he referred to as "motor mouth," had spilled her soul all over the break room table at the hospital, he replied, "Get away from me, you crazy cunt!" He was not about to take any money or go anywhere.

Carol then went to her apartment and began gathering evidence of the crimes. First, a bullet, which Doug had told Carol that was one of the bullets used in the murder of Gina Marano. He said the bullet had passed through Gina's head, and Carol thought the police could test it for Gina's blood to prove it had come from one of the guns she had purchased. She also grabbed a pair of panties Doug said had belonged to Gina. He had given Carol the bullet but kept the panties to wear himself.

Carol realized that where the victims had been found was in the jurisdiction of three different police departments, so it would be best if she notified all three. Phoning the operator to find out the individual precinct numbers, she dialed them one by one, only to get a busy signal each time. The operator refused to break in on any of the lines but did try one of the numbers herself.

It was the Northeast precinct, and Carol asked the detective who answered if he was familiar with the Sunset Strip murders. Of course he was. Was he familiar with a woman named Betsy/Claudia, she asked next? He was not sure. He would have to look through the case file again. Exasperated that the officer obviously did not recognize her, she just asked him if he wanted to be able to arrest the man behind the killings. He certainly would, he answered cautiously, not sure if this was some sick prank.

The detective had no clue what killings this woman was referencing and asked that she be more specific. She went on to tell him that he would need to contact Van Nuys and Burbank, as bodies had been dumped in their jurisdictions as well. He was then forced to ask her point-blank which killings she was referencing. That was all the encouragement Carol needed. She rattled off the crimes and stated her boyfriend was the one who was guilty, and she was afraid of him.

Asked why she had decided to come forward now, Carol said it was because she had finally committed a murder on her own and her boyfriend was very upset by it. Things had been bad for a while between the two, she stated, but ever since she had killed her other boyfriend, things had gone from bad to worse. She was sick of him treating her badly and just sick of the whole thing.

"Did she feel bad about the murders," the detective asked.

Her reply astounded him and is still startling. "The honest thing is," Carol answered truthfully. "It's fun to kill people, and if I was allowed to run loose, I'd probably do it again. I have to say— I know it's going to sound sick, it's going to sound psycho, and I really don't think I'm that psycho—but it's kind of fun. Like riding a roller coaster. Not the killing. Not the action that someone died because we did not kill them in a way that hurt them…"

Carol refused to give the detective Doug's name and voiced her worries that her boyfriend might kill her two sons if he found out she was speaking with police. That seems an odd accusation to make, considering that she had already spoken with Doug and notified him of her intention to go to the police.

Carol wanted to arrange a lunch meeting with the detectives from all three divisions at her favorite restaurant, Gristmill, the same restaurant she had overdosed in the parking lot. The detective asked if he could meet and talk with her before she notified the Van Nuys and Burbank precincts. Carol asked how long it would take him to get there, and he replied he was not entirely sure because his partner had the car, and he would have to wait for his return.

It seems ludicrous that you would have a self-professed killer on the phone wanting to turn herself in, and your reply is that you are unable to meet up with the subject. Surely someone could have given him a ride or considering the pressure the police were under to solve the Sunset Strip murders, it is almost certain his supervisor would have provided a car—hell, call a cab.

Inquiring how he would recognize her, Carol described to the detective the clothing she was wearing. Changing her clothing from her work scrubs into her street clothes before leaving the hospital had unintentionally allowed Carol to walk out of the building without drawing attention. She also told the detective she wore thick glasses because her eyesight was bad, and she often stumbled into things. Carol did not realize the shit storm she was about to stumble into.

While Carol was still on the phone, almost half a dozen police officers surrounded her apartment. They had been notified by an officer, who had responded to the hospital call, that Carol might be at home.

Meanwhile, police arrived at the Jergens factory to take Doug into custody. Doug was driven to the apartment he shared with Carol. When he saw the number of police officers swarming the building, sheer panic set in as a vice seemed to tighten its grip around his chest, making it difficult to breathe.

Doug wanted Carol out of the apartment before she turned anything over to police that would incriminate him in any crimes. He also feared that Carol's tendency to rattle on uncontrollably when she was nervous or excited would have negative consequences for him. Doug had known Carol long enough to realize that she relished being the center of attention.

It was a character flaw that Doug himself had used to manipulate Carol. Knowing that police would be clamoring for evidence and a statement from her, which would validate her claims, Doug sat handcuffed in the cruiser, sweating profusely in the

August heat. Doug needed a distraction to get the police officers' focus away from Carol and her crazy talk. He began yelling that Carol had a 12-gauge shotgun and might go crazy and blow everyone away.

Inside the apartment, Carol was fluttering around from one room to the other pressing evidence into the officers' hands while they looked on in shock and surprise. "Here, take this, it's a bullet from one of the murders and these are panties some of the victims were wearing when they were killed." Leading the police to the small room that Doug Clark used and stopped at a large filing cabinet, Carol unlocked the cabinet with a key and handed over the photo album containing the pictures of Shannon and Doug. Police had no idea if this woman was telling the truth or was just plain certifiable, but she certainly had their attention.

X
Criminal Psych Consideration

NO ONE, NOT EVEN THE MOST TRAINED AND adept psychologist, can know with unconditional certainty why one person becomes a serial killer while another does not. Study and speculation are the best means of insight the medical and legal fields are able to offer. Two people raised in virtually the same environment, with the same mitigating factors and predispositions, can still turn out completely differently. One individual might grow to become a person who is sympathetic to the plight of his fellow man and extremely adherent to the laws of the land, while the other commits selfish acts and crimes of atrocity with no apparent conscience.

Alan Carlisle, who the court tasked with performing a psychological evaluation of Ted Bundy, states the traumas endured by serial killers as children are generally the same as other children. It is up to the individual child, as they grow up, to decide how these instances affect and impact their decision-making. "It is not the traumas which create the killer," Carlisle states. "It's the manner in which he responds to them."

Carol Bundy grew up in a middle-class family in which both parents were abusive alcoholics. She was abused in every way possible and carried that abuse with her every day of her life, into each relationship and encounter. Many people have endured the same types of abuse and gone on to be upstanding individuals who would never inflict the suffering on others, which had been forced on them.

Doug Clark's family lived around the world, in places where their upper-middle-class status enabled them to have servants by the houseful. Doug developed a sense of entitlement and a feeling that he was superior to others—a trait that has been with him ever since. It is not known if Doug experienced any abuse either at the hands of his parents or anyone else. In fact, it seems, it was most often that Doug was the aggressor and the bully in situations.

It is also erroneously believed by most people that serial killers have no control over their urge to kill. Dennis Rader, aka "BTK", is proof that this is not true. Rader committed murders beginning in 1974 and committed his last murder in 1991. He evaded identification and capture until 2005. Rader told authorities he was able to suppress his desire to kill through mentally recalling details of the crimes while performing acts of autoeroticism.

Doug Clark grew visibly upset anytime the topic of necrophilia was brought up by investigators. If Doug had not participated in sexual acts with the deceased, as Carol Bundy insisted, then this is quite telling of Carol herself. Assuming for the moment that Clark was the killer that Carol states he was, but the necrophilic acts occurred only in Carol's mind, Carol immediately seems much more unhinged and perverted than her carefully crafted mousy demeanor indicates.

One begins to not only question the motive Carol had for making allegations regarding such a taboo subject, but also why Carol Bundy would even bring it up. What planted the seed in her mind in the first place? She alleged Doug would often bring up necrophilia during the conversations of their individual sexual fantasies. But it is entirely possible that Carol was the first to mention the topic. If we turn Carol's testimony around and reverse

Carol and Doug's roles in her statements, it is just as simple to believe she was the instigator.

It has already been established that Carol was an avid reader and enjoyed going to movies. From the time she was a young girl, books and movies had provided an escape for Carol into any world of her choosing. Her sister, Vicky, recalls an incident in which Carol sat calmly reading while she was being beaten with a belt. Carol had gone to see the movie *Caligula* about the famously hedonistic ruler who proudly committed murder, incest, and necrophilia. She had also greedily devoured a book on murderer and self-proclaimed necrophile, Ted Bundy.

Necrophilia, simply defined, means "love of the dead." There are a multitude of degrees and types of necrophilia. Many people have an attraction to the dark image the word evokes but would never consider having sexual intercourse with a person who was deceased. It is a misconception that female necrophiles do not exist and also that a deterrent to female necrophilia is the obvious problem involved with the deceased possessing a non-working phallus.

Three-quarters of women state they do not require penetration to achieve orgasm. That fact alone does away with the notion that phallic penetration by a partner, living or dead, is a factor in most women choosing a partner who makes them feel sexually fulfilled. Carol had seldom felt sexually fulfilled with her partners, and her pleasure was not a factor to her partners. She was merely an object to be used for their pleasure. It was her duty, and her pleasure was derived from the feeling that she had provided pleasure.

Beginning with the sexual acts her father forced upon her, Carol was never made to feel she had much of a choice, or that her feelings even merited thought. She stated she got more sexual pleasure from discussing murder, torture, and necrophilic acts with Doug Clark than she did when the two had sexual relations. Whether or not they were truthful is debatable, but several of Doug's former lovers took the stand at his trial and attested to his sexual prowess. If it is true that Doug was able to please other partners but not Carol, could it be a fault that lay within her?

A study by Rosman and Resnick in 1989, states the primary motive for necrophilic behavior is their overwhelming desire for "possession of an unresisting and unrejecting partner". This certainly sounds like Carol. Carol had a difficult time acquiring sexual partners, even her attempts to solicit prostitutes were often rebuffed.

Did Carol Bundy perform the necrophilic acts herself and transpose the events onto Doug Clark? It seems likely. Perhaps the washing of Exie Wilson's head was an attempt to remove any evidence that would tell investigators it was Carol and Jack who had played with the head. After all, the seminal fluid extracted from her throat matched Jack's blood type, not Doug's.

No matter if you believe the Doug/Carol or Jack/Carol scenario, the power dynamic involved in both couplings had similarities as well as parallels, which are hallmarks of serial killers. The need to control their victims, for instance. Whether the control is psychological, sexual, or financial in nature, the control impulse is always present. What the abuser gains from his victim can also be psychological, sexual pleasure, or financial gain.

Jack Murray controlled Carol Bundy through financial circumstances. He made sure Carol realized that were it not for him, she would not have gotten as much as she did from the sale of her house, she would not have the social security payments or even the surgery to partially restore her vision to allow her to return to work. By making Carol feel that she owed him, Carol would then feel that she was obligated to hand over money to him at his request.

Doug Clark was essentially controlled by Carol Bundy through financial circumstances. She knew that his job would not support the lifestyle he wanted to live. He would be unable to spend the money he wanted at bars, and on the women that he met in those bars, and still afford rent on his own apartment. When he moved into Carol Bundy's apartment, he did not even own a car, and his request when she changed apartments was that it be close to work, so he could ride his motorcycle. Carol gifted Doug with clothing, watches, anything she thought would make him happy, while at the same time keeping him dependent on her. He might have called her a "cow" when she upset him, but Doug had to have known she was more like a "cash cow."

There seemed to be a constant and ongoing power struggle between both "couples." All were involved in BDSM, which requires one party to be dominant while the other is submissive. One cannot exist without the other, and in a way, both people retain control. Although most couples who participate in BDSM achieve fulfillment and pleasure from their roles, that was not the case among these three people. There were too much ego and narcissism and not enough humility.

These were not healthy relationships and never would be because the people in them were not mentally healthy. All three wanted to be in control, and when it became apparent that no one was willing to back down from their bid for power, the obvious answer was to seek out people they could control. The more out-of-control Carol, Doug, and Jack felt, the more urgent their desire to control became.

XI
Inadmissible & Erroneous Evidence

THE EVIDENCE THE PROSECUTION AND LAW enforcement used to convict Doug Clark, and the testimony of Carol Bundy, should be measured against two facts: both parties were pathological liars, and with the possibility of the death sentence looming before them, it is not surprising they each participated in constant and carefully constructed finger-pointing. Even after Carol was assured via her plea bargain that she could not be sentenced to the death penalty, she continued to make wildly impossible and unsubstantiated accusations.

Carol Bundy's account made this an even more confusing and distorted case. Carol had given a confession to the police on numerous occasions in which she repeatedly changed her story. Even though these were things Carol presented as fact, when told by the police that she had information, such as a particular date, wrong, she was allowed to retract and amend her statement. Carol told one story when she phoned police to turn herself in, another during her testimony for the plea agreement, and yet another completely different third version at trial. She was unpredictable, and therefore, unreliable witness, and yet the state hung the entirety of their case on her words.

Carol had placed a call to police two days after the Marano-Chandler murders in which she implicated her lover and claimed to have firsthand knowledge of the crimes he had related to her, as well as evidence from the crime scene. Carol claimed the killer described how he had seen Gina and Cynthia, who he referred to as "the twins," and recognized Cynthia as a prostitute he had picked up on prior occasions. No one else besides Carol would suggest that either one or both of the girls were prostitutes.

Carol went on to state that Doug was not physically attracted to Gina, but he had been unable to talk Cynthia into coming along with him, so both girls got in the car, and he took them to a secluded location. Cynthia was going to perform fellatio on Doug, and he told Gina to look away. When she did, Doug shot her in the head. Cynthia panicked, and Doug shot her in the head as well. Noticing Gina had not succumbed to her head wound, Doug shot her in the head again before turning the gun on Cynthia again, shooting her in the chest.

According to Carol, Doug then loaded the girls' bodies into the car and drove to a garage he rented. Dragging the bodies inside, he stripped them, placed the girls in a simulated 69 position for mutual oral sex, and used his Polaroid to take photos. He next committed acts of necrophilia, ejaculating into Gina's anus and Cynthia's vagina, before taking them to the site where their bodies were found.

At the time of autopsy, however, no semen was found other than a small amount outside Cynthia's vagina. There were no signs of force being used, such as bruising or tears in the tissue, no pubic hairs, or any other evidence of sexual activity, which can be difficult to determine when the victim is deceased. The minimal amount of semen collected from the outside of Cynthia's vulva was blood typed—DNA testing not yet being available—and the blood type came back as belonging to Jack Murray, not Doug Clark.

Nothing Carol reported to police could be substantiated. No evidence pointed to Doug being the killer. The facts Carol stated were incorrect, but the police pressed on, feeling they were making great strides in the case.

The condition of the bodies indicated they had been thrown from a moving vehicle. This would seem to indicate two people were involved. One person was needed to drive the vehicle while the other person busied themselves pushing the girls' bodies out. If this were true, then Carol's statement that Doug committed the acts by himself is inarguably false.

As with the lack of any forensic evidence in the Marano-Chandler murders linking Doug to the crimes, the facts Carol gave to the police about what she had witnessed in regard to Exie Wilson also appeared false. Stating that she had entered the apartment—in various accounts, Carol changes the details of the discovery—to discover Doug had been keeping Exie's decapitated head in the freezer.

After giving the head a makeover by applying her own cosmetics, Carol says she stood back to admire her handiwork, and Doug Clark seized the head, announcing he was taking it in the shower with him. When Carol inquired why, Doug reportedly replied to have oral sex with it. He then disappeared into the bathroom and returned sometime later, verbally confirming he had committed necrophilia.

The first question that comes to mind is how Doug was able to achieve this. The police stated Exie's head was a solid piece of ice, and the mouth had been frozen shut. Even though it had been exposed to the Los Angeles heat for several hours before discovery, the head remained frozen. When the medical examiner performed his exam the next day, he reported that the brain had been a mixture of frozen tissue and icy slush, which he had difficulty excising. The only seminal fluid recovered, once the head had thawed, again does not match Doug Clark's blood type, but that of Jack Murray.

Can the possibility be ruled out that the head was not completely frozen if and when Doug had sex with it? Could Doug have used the head in the act of simulated fellatio and not ejaculated? Both of these things are possible. They are not, however, probable. It sounds more like a story invented by a wild imagination with the hope of making Doug look even more like a monster. If he could commit such perverted acts with the dead, then surely, he was capable of anything.

This is not to say Doug Clark sits on Death Row as a man completely innocent of any wrongdoing. Without a doubt, he was a child molester—the most despicable sort of human slime imaginable. It's understandable why people feel Doug Clark should never be given the opportunity to walk the streets and feel the sunshine on his face. That is a privilege he has lost and should never again be granted. The evidence used to convict him of murder, however, is farcical and flawed at best.

We really have very little to go on other than Carol Bundy's finger-pointing. In almost every single one, if not all, the murders, the gun used was the .25 caliber Raven, which Carol had indicated to police belonged to her. It was Carol who bought the two handguns, and it was Carol's makeup bag in which both of the guns were found, having been located after the couple was taken into custody.

Doug states that once the police started looking into the murder of Jack Murray, Carol told him to hide the guns. Why he would follow any instructions from Carol, something completely outside the norm for him, he has no logical explanation for. A coworker of Doug's discovered the hidden weapons when he lost his footing while doing his rounds. As he reached out in search of a handhold, his hand brushed against the fabric makeup bag. Pulling it from where it had been tucked away, and unzipping it, he was shocked to see there were two handguns.

Among information seemingly suppressed by police, was that Jack Murray was also in possession of two handguns. The police learned from Jeanette during the investigation into his homicide that Jack had purchased two unregistered guns illegally. Jack's immigration status prevented him from legally purchasing and owning firearms. One of the guns police discovered was a nine-millimeter. The other was a small-caliber handgun that fired the same type of bullets used to commit the Sunset Strip murders.

Strangely, although the nine-millimeter would make it into the police evidence locker, the other handgun, the one that could have either proven or disproven Jack's involvement in the crimes, disappeared. The paper trail, which indicates the police were ever in possession of the gun, seems to lead to a dead end. Paperwork shows that Jack's wife Jeanette told police about the existence of both guns, but the appearance of a police cover-up, even if it were only to cover up the fact they had lost or misplaced the weapon, leads credence to the idea that police conspired to alter evidence. Especially given that the officer in charge of the search was accused of altering a witness testimony and perjury during the trial.

The evidence that Doug had worried about the most, the photo album containing Polaroids of himself with Shannon, would be ruled inadmissible. Carol had produced the album for police from a locked cabinet inside the room Doug used as his own. The judge ruled the search warrant would not cover the discovery. Doug never had to answer for his role in the molestation of Shannon.

One of the complaints Doug still raises is that, in 1980, he was illegally detained and questioned by police without his Miranda rights being read and without legal representation. At the time, Doug had not been officially charged with the crimes in question, and was, therefore, not technically under arrest. He came into the police station voluntarily and answered questions of his own free will.

It was more a case of Doug being suspected of having information about criminal activity, rather than being a person that the police were naming as a suspect in the commission of these crimes. So if he, in fact, asked for representation and his request was ignored, had law enforcement actually denied him his Constitutional Rights? This is dicey territory.

Looking back at an event that occurred almost forty years ago, it is imperative to remember that revisions to laws are constantly being made, and each state has its own statutes. Depending on the crime that a person is suspected of committing, the length of time they can be held without formal arrest charges varies.

For example, a person suspected of terrorism can be held for up to two weeks without any official charges being filed. If the police were not charging Doug with murder at that time, they had the right to question him as to any knowledge he might have, and he had the right to refuse to answer those questions.

Doug Clark knew damn good and well that he did not have to say a word. In all likelihood, he had already begun laying the groundwork for a strategy that he hoped would result in a mistrial. Despite his swagger and protestations to the opposite, Doug Clark is afraid to die.

XII

Trial & Error

HAVING SIGNED A PLEA AGREEMENT STATING that in exchange for her testimony against Doug Clark, the state of California would not pursue the death penalty against her, Carol Bundy happily took the witness stand, feeling like she had nothing to lose. Carol, a witness for the prosecution, had been writing letters to Doug in prison in which she encouraged him to do whatever he had to do, including lie about her involvement, in order to save his own skin.

his trial date approached, Doug Clark became more dissatisfied with his legal representation and more convinced a jury would not convict him. The only person claiming to be an actual witness to the crimes was Carol Bundy, who had frequently changed her story to fit the timeline of events. No fingerprints or other forensic evidence belonging to Doug was found at the crime scenes. The only seminal fluid recovered from the victims was not a match to Doug Clark. There was nothing to link him directly to the crimes, so all of the evidence the prosecution planned to introduce was circumstantial.

Positive that a reasonable jury would never believe Carol, Doug nonetheless began to gather his own evidence. Witnesses were willing to testify that they had either been with or seen Doug at the time prosecutors alleged he was out committing murder. He also had receipts and canceled checks that showed he was not in the vicinity of the murder victims.

It took over two years from the time Doug was arrested and charged with the murders for his case to come to trial, but it finally began in October 1982. Although he had learned a great deal about the legal process while awaiting trial, Doug repeatedly damaged his own cause with temper tantrums, outbursts, and arguments with the judge.

Doug felt that the defense lawyer assigned to him was not equipped to launch an adequate defense and requested the judge assign a different attorney. He was never satisfied with any of the defense lawyers, especially one in particular who came to court smelling of alcohol and had a habit of falling asleep during court proceedings.

Lunchtime was spent by the defense attorney at a nearby bar, where he proceeded to drink his lunch. The records indicate that a bailiff even complained to the presiding judge that the defense attorney showed up each morning reeking of liquor so strongly it almost floored the officer of the court. The judge took the matter under advisement and ruled that the trial proceed as scheduled.

Doug continued to loudly voice his dissatisfaction with the defense lawyers assigned to his case. He went through several attorneys, and the lineup for the defense seemed to be in a constant state of rotation similar to a revolving door. Railing to the judge about how unqualified and inept one lawyer was and making accusations that another was showing up to court drunk, Doug made the request to represent himself. He seemed to think if he protested loudly enough, it would buy him a mistrial.

A defendant always has the option of self-representation unless a judge feels the defendant's mental state or capacity would not allow them to adequately represent themselves, or if the judge feels they have any other valid reason to deny them this right. Doug had certainly studied the law enough while awaiting his trial to be capable of acting as his own attorney, but the accused who chooses self-representation is also supposed to be allowed access to a law library and assistance of a co-counsel.

The judge presiding over Doug's trial was unwilling to let him use the law library, perhaps because Ted Bundy, who had been acting as his own attorney, had recently escaped from custody through the window of a courthouse where he had been left unattended to study his notes while the bailiff went off to take a smoke break. The judge also went on to tell Doug that if he did not believe he could adequately represent himself alone, without co-counsel, then it would be best for Doug to retain the services of the attorney who had been assigned to represent him and forget self-representation.

Viewing this as a criticism of his intelligence, Doug used a few choice curse words to tell the judge what he thought of his opinion. Doug did himself no favor in regard to the impression his attitude and behavior made on the jury. His best bet, in his opinion, was to be honest—brutally honest—about Shannon and about anything else he felt the prosecution might use against him.

If he could manage to beat them to the punch and admit he had committed a crime with this child, but he was not a murderer, he felt the court would have a more favorable impression of him. Odd that it would occur to someone that being a child molester would save them from the death penalty and make them seem less evil than the crimes they stood accused of committing.

As it turned out, the prosecution was unable to charge Doug with child molestation, and the plans he had crafted were not necessary. He would not have to publicly acknowledge in open court that he was a child molester only because the evidence was deemed inadmissible and the charges unrelated to the murder charges. There was no justice for Shannon.

A woman named Charlene Andermann had come forward with allegations that Doug Clark had assaulted her and stabbed her with a knife, in an attempt to kill her. Charlene was the only person to state that she knew Doug to be her attacker, and the prosecution was hopeful her testimony would lend weight and credence to the charges levied against the defendant. Police had been first alerted to the story of Charlene's attack in a phone call the spring preceding Doug's trial.

Carol had placed the phone call to Robbery/Homicide reporting she had heard a rumor that a woman incarcerated in the same facility had been spreading around a story about fighting for her life with Doug Clark. Police traveled to the lockup and interviewed Charlene, where she was shown a photo lineup of suspects. They found her story to be credible enough that upon their recommendation, the prosecution would use her as a witness.

When called to the witness stand to share her story, Charlene testified that around ten in the evening on April 27, 1980, she was on Sunset Boulevard when she was approached by a white male she identified as Doug Clark, who was driving a blue station wagon with wood side panels. She stated that the defendant solicited her for oral sex. Upon coming to an agreement on a price for the act, she then entered the car through the passenger side. Next, she said Doug took hold of her and suddenly began stabbing her repeatedly in the back, neck, arms, chest, and stomach. Doctors were able to count twenty-six separate wounds.

During the struggle, Charlene had been able to grab the knife, but it was the blade of the knife that she managed to wrap her hand around. As she pulled the knife towards her in an attempt to wrench it away from her attacker, the blade severed the tendons in her hand. At one point, she said, "Mister, that's blood. You're hurtin' me."

Doug merely laughed, Charlene told the court, and said, "I know." She was finally able to open the car door and escape. Bleeding profusely, she would end up in the hospital for her injuries. Police planned on having Charlene brought to the police department, where she would be asked to identify her attacker in an actual police lineup.

When Doug was informed that he was to appear in the lineup, he told them to kiss his ass. It was rumored that Charlene had identified another individual at the lineup in which Doug had refused to participate. Because of this, Charlene might not have initially seemed a particularly credible witness, yet when she took the stand, Charlene identified Doug Clark as the man who had attempted to kill her. She knew beyond a shadow of a doubt that he was her attacker because she would never forget those cold eyes.

Several factors aided the defense with being able to have these allegations and charges thrown out of court and the witness discredited. Not only had she identified separate individuals as her attacker, but the vehicle she said the assailant was driving did not fit the description of any of the vehicles Doug had access to. The defense also told the court that Charlene had changed the date of the attack and where she had been when the perpetrator picked her up more than once.

Perhaps most damaging to her testimony was when she was asked if it was true that she was under the influence of narcotics at the time of the assault as well as the time she had identified her attacker. Charlene was forced to admit she did use street drugs as well as alcohol. Charlene burst into tears and attempted an explanation. She was dismissed from the witness stand, and the charges were dropped.

The prosecution had only two things they felt would get them a conviction against Doug Clark; Carol's testimony and circumstantial evidence, and Doug knew it. In Carol's confession to police, she had brought up the garage in which she stated Doug told her he had participated in necrophilia with the Marano and Chandler bodies. She had stated that after Doug told her about the murders and the mess that he made dragging the bodies across the garage floor, she traveled with him to the garage and assisted with cleaning up blood and other evidence.

When police searched the garage, they did not find the evidence Carol had described, nor proof it ever looked as she said it had. It was clear the floor had not been scrubbed to remove blood stains or anything else. In fact, judging by the amount of dirt, dust, and debris on the floor, it seemed the floor had never been swept, let alone scrubbed as Carol claimed.

A footprint was observed, however, and law enforcement felt they had to make a choice between preserving the print for later comparison or performing a presumptive test for blood, which would destroy the print. They opted to perform the test for blood and reported the test gave them a result that indicated the source was *likely* blood. If they were to say the test showed it was *definitely* blood, then the defense could have asked them to provide the results of further testing performed to back up that statement, tests they neither performed nor had results from.

Why had the police not taken photographs of the boot print, and then performed the testing that would provide a definitive answer as to the presence of blood? That's a good question that has never been satisfactorily answered. Maybe they were simply aware in a case where they had only been able to produce shaky and circumstantial evidence; it was best not to leave any room for further doubt.

While Doug was seated with law enforcement during questioning, one of the officers made the observation the boots Doug was wearing appeared to be the same tread as the print they had found in the garage. During the trial, Doug said it only made sense that boots he owned left prints in the garage he rented. "What the fuck am I supposed to do, levitate around my garage?" Doug asked sarcastically. The boots in question were thoroughly tested and did not reveal ever having been in contact with any blood.

Another point of contention that Doug brought up at trial was a portrait that had been stored in his garage and later hung in Carol Bundy's apartment. When Carol had contacted the police to turn herself in, she pointed out to law enforcement that on the back of the painting were minuscule drops of what Doug had bragged to her was Gina Marano's blood.

The most the crime lab had been able to tell police was that the blood appeared to be the same blood type as Gina's. Drawing his witness out on the stand, Doug asked if it was possible the blood had been kept somewhere by the killer before placing it on the picture. Could the killer have stored the blood in a refrigerator until he or she had the opportunity to put it on the item? It was possible, the expert conceded. That was all Doug wanted to hear.

Doug knew the importance of giving the jury a small grain of reasonable doubt. Just a tiny bit, just a nibble, enough to say that they could not say with absolute certainty that Doug Clark was guilty of the murders. Given the facts and with permission by the judge to enter into evidence some of the items Doug possessed, which helped establish his alibi, as well as cast suspicion on Jack, a competent defense lawyer should have, at least, be capable of getting a declaration of a mistrial.

Doug would try on multiple occasions to convince the jury that Carol's version of events did not fit the evidence. Carol stated that when Exie Wilson's head was disposed of, she had bought the wooden box, and while Doug was driving, she followed his instructions to toss it out of the car. She could distinctly remember the sound of it hitting the ground as well as the rear passenger side tire running over it.

No matter which car Carol claimed they were in at the time, her Buick station wagon or her Datsun compact, it would have been virtually impossible for the low-slung vehicles to drive over the box. It was Doug's contention that Carol was with Murray in his van, and that the van ran over the box.

Some of the crimes seemed to mimic those of Ted Bundy, the Manson Family, and other killers. A book about Ted Bundy had hit store shelves a year prior to the Sunset Strip murders. Carol was an avid reader and especially enjoyed true crime. Perhaps she truly *had* attempted to emulate some of her heroes. Maybe a lifetime of being made to feel she was inferior and not good enough finally caused her to feel she needed to prove she was capable of doing anything a man could do—including murder.

The jury began its deliberations in February 1983, and by this time, Doug's screaming and name-calling had destroyed any credibility he may have had in the eyes of the jury. No one would soon forget the sight of a manacled Doug Clark, who the judge had ordered to be gagged if he wished to remain in the courtroom. The leather gag placed over his mouth by a court bailiff had little effect, and Doug was still able to shout a muffled but clearly discernible, "fuck you" at the judge. Being reminded once again that he would not be allowed to remain if he continued to cause a disruption, Doug was soon quieted by the quick-thinking bailiff who slapped a women's sanitary napkin over the gag.

It would take the jury five days to reach a unanimous verdict. At the end of the first day, only two jurors were in favor of acquittal, the majority believing the prosecution had easily met its requisite burden of proof. For the remaining few days, they would review all of the evidence presented during the trial. They all felt that Carol Bundy was a credible, if somewhat pathetic, witness, who was just one of many women over whom Doug Clark had exerted control.

Doug's ability to turn on the charm and his intelligence had, at first, taken in some of the jurors, but his behavior during the trial, and his abusive treatment of his defense attorney, as well as the presiding judge, made jury members feel it was all merely performance for their benefit. Taking these matters into consideration, along with the prosecution's evidence, and Doug's lies in the courtroom, made it clear to them that Doug was guilty. Their verdict was announced to the courtroom that same day. Doug looked over his shoulder to where his mother sat nervously, awaiting the jury's decision on her son's fate, smiled, winked at her, and said, "Hi, Mom."

The penalty phase of Doug's trial was a chance for both sides to present any evidence that had not been allowed during the trial. It was an important period for Doug, as it would be determined whether he would go to the gas chamber. Doug's parents were questioned, and both of them denied any knowledge of behavioral problems in Doug's early life.

Dr. Gloria E. Keyes, who had spent over one hundred hours interviewing and evaluating Doug Clark, took the stand and gave her professional opinion and results of the psychiatric exam she had performed. Doug had opposed her being allowed to testify and would object over small details throughout her testimony during both of the days she was on the witness stand. Perhaps what bothered Doug the most was that Dr. Keyes' evaluation seemed so apparently on target.

The doctor testified that Doug was a narcissist, who manifested delusions of grandeur by putting other people down. She went on to say that Doug was unable to relate to others. He also had what she termed, "antisocial personality traits," which included impulsivity, social-norm deviation, and job performance problems. His job performance problems were evidenced by his inability to retain a job for an extended period of time. He did not deal well with authority figures, feeling he should not be receiving orders, but instead be giving orders to others.

The doctor also stated that Doug had a personality disorder with low self-esteem, psychosexual disorder, and paranoia. He possessed a strong denial that there was anything wrong with him.

After Dr. Keyes finished providing the court with her diagnosis, Doug insisted that the court allow him to approach and question her while she was still on the witness stand. Doug's defense counsel strongly advised against him questioning the doctor for fear that he would further prove her point. Doug questioned the doctor against his co-defense attorney's advice and soon found himself agreeing to many points the doctor made. During his own testimony, Doug's explanation of his belief in his own superiority over anyone who had been in a position of authority during his life, including the lawyers in the courtroom, went right along with what the good doctor had said. Doug was quickly losing ground.

The prosecutor felt that with the right set of questions, Doug Clark would talk himself right into the death penalty. He was right. The death penalty was given to Doug Clark for all six counts of murder. While still on Death Row, Doug married a heavy-set woman by the name of Kelly Keniston. She would vehemently and publicly protest her husband's innocence. Doug would continue to use every legal avenue available to avoid execution.

The day that Carol Bundy was scheduled to go to trial on the charges against her, she chose to withdraw her plea of not guilty by reason of insanity and instead pleaded guilty to both charges of murder in the first degree. She would eventually be sentenced to two consecutive terms of twenty-five years to life in state prison, plus an additional two years for the illegal use of a gun. It was the maximum sentence the court could give her because the plea agreement she had entered into with prosecutors meant she could not be sentenced to the death penalty.

She would continue to support Doug Clark in his fight to prove his innocence, even though he would continue to discredit her. In 1990, she handed over all of her legal and psychiatric files to Doug's lawyers to help him to do so. When asked why she still wanted to help Doug, she would say she still liked him, although she could not say why. She instructed him to do and say whatever it took to gain his freedom.

If Doug took Carol up on her offer, then we will certainly never know if the things he attests to are true or if they were lies manufactured by Carol and himself in a bid for his freedom. Carol gloried over the feeling of power she had by handing over her life to Doug to do with it as he chose. She would, in her mind, appear the sacrificial martyr who was giving up her freedom and her life for her man. Secretly, it made her feel as if she were the dominant figure.

Conclusion

I AM FULLY AWARE THAT THE PUBLICATION OF this book will be met with criticism of not only my writing but also the motive behind it. There will be allegations I am merely one of many who have attempted to profit from this story. It will be said this book is another in a long list of books and articles that distorts facts.

I readily admit I am not the world's best writer, and that knowledge alone shows that if my motives were solely for financial gain, it would be a poor strategy. I have made a lifelong study of criminals and criminal psychology and have a strong desire to understand what motivates criminals. I will never empathize or come to a complete understanding of the workings of the criminal mind, and for that, I am grateful.

I write with an awareness that the crimes are like pebbles tossed in the water whose ripples continue on and spread over the years. The pain victims and their families, as well as the pain the convicted person's family experiences, does not end when the story is no longer front-page news. The memories are not forgotten just because the guilty person is locked away out of the harsh media glare.

Above all, I attempt to always write with respect for the victims and those affected by the crimes. There is still much to learn about the workings of the criminal mind, as well as how to identify people who have certain traits, which, once recognized, might help prevent you from becoming a victim yourself. I firmly believe, just as the philosopher George Santayana said, "Those who cannot remember the past are condemned to repeat it."

The fact that two of the key players in this story, Carol Bundy and Jack Murray, are long dead, and Doug Clark has been on Death Row for over a quarter of a decade has not stopped nor slowed down the debates and speculations regarding who is actually guilty. Doug Clark is seventy years old at the time this is being written and more likely to die on Death Row from natural causes rather than the gas chamber. Either way, when he dies, all the stories and the victims will again be dredged up and served to the masses.

Carol Mary Bundy was pronounced dead December 9, 2003, after being hospitalized for heart and respiratory issues, as well as complications from diabetes. The months leading up to her death were filled with frequent hospitalizations as her health diminished rapidly. There are many people who feel cheated by not having the opportunity to witness her death.

A family member of one of the Sunset Strip victims was bitterly disappointed that Carol was allowed to choose her own fate by becoming a witness for the prosecution and, thereby, dodging the death penalty. Carol's victims were not given a chance to decide when and where they would die. The victim's family member at least takes comfort in their personal belief that Carol will pay for her crimes by burning in hell for all of eternity.

One of Carol's fellow inmates remembers the way other prisoners would torment Carol. "As time went by, Carol was almost totally blind from her diabetes." The woman goes on to describe the way inmates would attack Carol physically, knowing that she could neither see the attack coming nor know who her attacker was. "She lived in constant fear inside her dark world," the woman who wishes to remain anonymous states. "I believe that was her own personal hell. She died in pain from the diabetic sores and was blind. It was what she deserved."

That might not be justice enough for some of the victim's families, but it is the only justice they will get when it comes to Carol Bundy. There will never be any further confessions or apologies. Doug Clark no longer has the hope that someday Carol will admit she wrongfully accused him. That hope died with Carol Bundy when she died. He still hopes that evidence will vindicate him, and he will be exonerated of all charges and someday walk out of prison a free man, while he is still actually able to walk. Otherwise, he feels he will leave prison the same way Carol left prison—feet first and horizontal.

In just one of many odd and bizarre footnotes to this story, Doug was featured with three fellow serial killers for an article in Vanity Fair magazine. The four serial killers, dubbed the "San Quentin Bridge Club", met on a regular basis for cards and testosterone-fueled debates. Not about who was the most prolific killer among the four, but who was the best bridge player and who was the best cheater.

There will never be closure for many of the families out there. Doug Clark had been charged with and convicted of six murders, but police said he was suspected of committing at least twenty-five murders. Where this precise number comes from, the police are unwilling to discuss. By making a statement like that, the families of the women who remain missing or whose bodies were perhaps found, but families were not notified because there was no way of identifying them, just leave families wondering if he murdered their loved one.

Gina and Cynthia's sister still lives with the fact that her beloved sisters were murdered through no fault of their own, possibly sexually assaulted while they lay dying or shortly thereafter and labeled erroneously as teen prostitutes. I cannot say why Doug and Carol stated the girls were prostitutes, except that perhaps they felt their actions would seem less horrific, if not justifiable, to jurors who might feel that hookers got what they deserved by choosing such a dangerous lifestyle. I have never felt that prostitutes are somehow less than human, nor will I ever think it. These girls were nevertheless not prostitutes. They were teenagers. Teenagers who were seeking freedom and the meaning of life. Teenagers who were still discovering who they were and who they wanted to be. There is no way of telling what great accomplishments both would have gone on to make. Their family can now only speculate. Gina and Cynthia did not have the opportunity to graduate, meet their true love, or raise a family. Their future was stolen from them. That makes this crime unforgivable.

Shannon was only a child and a pawn at the hands of these monsters. The fear and the pain that she has lived with all these years, in itself, is criminal. The strength of her character, the fortitude within her, has made her the survivor she is today. Doug Clark, especially, set out to ruin Shannon's childhood and eventually rob her not only of that but also of her life as well.

If you want to credit Carol Bundy in small part with saving Shannon's life by her decision to turn Doug over to the authorities before he was able to carry out his plot to murder Shannon, that's fine, but never let that outshine the fact that Shannon has chosen not to let these crimes prevent her from living. Her innocence and security were stolen. These are not tangible items like a television set. Tangible items can be restored or replaced. Innocence and security, once taken, cannot be fully restored, no matter how many years pass or how many hours of therapy the victim undergoes.

To the families of both Doug Clark and Carol Bundy, who have lived nearly forty years with the stigma of being related to these two, I have a genuine sympathy for you. I cannot fathom how much pain and ridicule you have endured.

Jack Murray's family has been mostly ignored, which is a blessing and a curse. His children have been victims of the secrets he kept during his life, and his death as a murder victim himself only offers further pain and questions. There is no resolution and no answers. You have not been forgotten. Jack helped many people in his time on this earth. Hold on to the good.

With writing this book, it is my fervent desire that we can hopefully not only prevent future crimes by learning more about the inner workings of the criminal mind, but also the changes that could be made in our justice system. It is not my intention to explain away or justify any criminal acts; rather, I have pointed out flaws in the legal system because all too often, the guilty party evades justice because of these legal loopholes. At times, it feels as if the system protects the criminals more often than the victims.

I am not here to push my values and beliefs on others. Part of my reason for writing this book is also to allow people to draw logical deductions and conclusions by studying the circumstances. I fully encourage readers to research criminal cases on their own, so they can then form an educated opinion.

My hope is that everyone who has been touched by the string of crimes that occurred in 1980 is able to eventually find some modicum of peace. I have related the facts as they have been told to me, in addition to the trial transcripts and other official documents

I ploddingly sifted through. I have drawn my own conclusions, and now I leave it up to readers to draw their own.

Acknowledgments

This is a special thanks to the following readers who have taken time out of their busy schedule to be part of the True Crime Seven Team. Thank you all so much for all the feedback and support!

JS, Evette Richards, Evette White, Ohpa, Muhammad Nizam Bin Mohtar, Tammy Marshall, Jessica Janus, Tim Garris, Vicki Gordon, Angie Leblanc, Robin Leigh Morgan, Magra Dearest, Jennifer L. Varga, Natalie G. Spearman, Dark Angel NV, Bob Ayers, Allyssa, Lisa, Susan Groth, Marcia Jenkins, Elizabeth A Norris, JS, Diane Hogberg, Pamela John, Elmer Lang, Lular

Continue Your Exploration Into

The Murderous Minds

Excerpt From Murderous Minds Volume 1

I
Michael David Clagett

MICHAEL D. CLAGETT SAW THE PRISON GUARDS approaching his cell. It was time.

One guard unlocked the cell door, and two other guards secured him in handcuffs and leg shackles. Clagett exchanged a few words with them as they started walking in silence toward the room of the corrections center where his execution would take place.

For Clagett, the brief walk down the cold, sterile hallways of the Greensville Correction Center seemed to take forever. It was not because he dreaded what awaited him. On the contrary, Clagett welcomed his execution.

He was offered two options for his execution; lethal injection or the electric chair. He chose the electric chair. He thought it was ironic. He felt he deserved to die; yet, around twenty people had gathered outside the prison to hold a candlelight vigil. The gathering was organized by Virginians for Alternatives to the Death Penalty. They sang songs and read passages from the Bible.

The thirty-nine-year-old Clagett would be the second inmate executed by electric chair since the state of Virginia passed a law offering inmates a choice. He had been on death row for six years and was serving five death sentences, one for each person he had killed on June 30, 1994.

His trial ended with the jury convicting him of four counts of capital murder in the commission of a robbery, along with one count of multiple homicide murder.

As the guards led him into the room where his execution would take place, he saw a small group of people, some family members of his victims, seated in the viewing room. They would witness his execution. Some were standing. Two of those standing were his mother and his wife Karen, who he had married while on death row. Both were in tears. Though he fully accepted his fate, he would die with unanswered questions; why did he do it? Why did he allow his girlfriend, Denise, talk him into killing those people?

Power Play

Denise Holsinger separated from her husband, Randell Holsinger, in 1993, and met Clagett soon after. Clagett was everything her husband was not. While her husband was a first-class petty officer in the Navy, Clagett was chronically unemployed, had a history of committing domestic violence, and a long history of drinking and using drugs. She had her own demons and engaged in drinking and drug use. She had three children, whom she left with her husband as she did not feel she could deal with the responsibility. She just wanted out, and Clagett appealed to her because of his wild streak. She'd grown tired of being the proper Navy wife. Clagett's irresponsible manner provided the freedom to express her discontent with life.

Holsinger met Clagett at her place of work, the Witchduck Inn. Located on Pembroke Boulevard, in Virginia Beach, Witchduck Inn is a tavern and restaurant, and Clagett was a regular there. Clagett frequented the tavern so often that he considered the bar owner, Lam Van Son, a friend. Son had fled his native South

Vietnam during the communist takeover. He had fought with U.S. soldiers, as he was part of South Vietnam's Special Forces unit.

When South Vietnam fell to the communist in 1975, Son was placed in a re-education camp. Son escaped the camp and traveled to Thailand by boat before coming to America. He had settled in Lynchburg, where he married Lanna Le Son in 1988.

Holsinger rented a small apartment, and Clagett moved in with her. He spent most of the time lying around the house getting stoned. Holsinger would join him when she arrived home from work. While Clagett did not contribute to the household, Holsinger allowed it.

It put her in a position where she felt she held power in the relationship, and that power came without resistance. In her marriage, she felt she had to play the role of the dutiful wife; it was different with Clagett. In their relationship, she was the one with the job and the money, and she was the one who offered him female attention.

Terminated

It was in June of 1994, the demons within Holsinger and Clagett collided to create an explosion of violence that sent the community into shock. Holsinger had been pocketing money from her job at the Witchduck Inn. She had been doing it for months; to help support the drug habit that had begun to consume both her and Clagett.

Unfortunately for Holsinger, her stealing caught up with her. Her boss, Lam Van Son, caught on to what she was doing and fired her June 28. Holsinger was livid when Son told her that he was letting her go. Instead of being grateful that Son was not going to report her crime to the police, Holsinger cursed him and blamed him for being paranoid about the whole thing. She insisted she was innocent.

Giving in

Holsinger arrived home after work to find Clagett in the living room, inhaling from a bong. He also had a bottle of whiskey. Holsinger grabbed the bong and took a few puffs before drinking from the bottle. She told Clagett about being fired as the drugs and alcohol took effect. Clagett reached out to comfort her but she pushed him away. She was determined she was going to make Son pay.

Clagett got up from the couch and took her in his arms, telling her it would be all right; somehow, they would make it. Clagett's attempts to console her were not working; he could see that she remained upset. He thought he knew what would help. He ran his drunk, stoned hands all over her before pulling her into the bedroom. They had wild and intense sex; the kind he knew would get her to release the pressure she kept inside.

The next morning, as the two of them lay in bed, Holsinger divulged her plan. She wanted Clagett with her when she robbed the Witchduck. She stroked his chest and told him after they got the money, they could get away and find a new place to live.

She had ideas of going to Mexico or Canada. Clagett seemed hesitant in agreeing to her plan. The worst offense he was ever jailed for was committing domestic violence against his last two wives. Because of the brutality of his crimes, he had been jailed for several years. Still, he wanted to please Holsinger. She convinced him by comparing them to Bonnie and Clyde. They would be free and famous.

He wanted Holsinger's approval. It led him to agree. In his mind, Clagett had nothing to lose and everything to gain. For the next two days, the couple would binge on drugs and alcohol.

The Witchduck Assault

On June 30, thirty-one-year-old Karen Rounds arrived for her shift at the Witchduck Inn. She had been hired by Son to replace Holsinger as their new waitress. A Pennsylvania native, Rounds moved to Virginia Beach with her husband, Kevin Rounds.

Rounds had been a nurse but looking for a career change. She had worked as a nurse at a state prison while her husband was in the Navy. When they moved to Virginia Beach, she got a job working at the Maryview Medical Center; a clinic located in Churchland. She quit her job to go back to school to study computers.

Her new job at the Witchduck Inn would provide her with some spending money while attending classes. Both Karen and her husband knew Clagett as they often saw him when they went to Witchduck. Karen found Clagett to be creepy, but her husband had reassured her that he would not harm anyone.

When she entered the Witchduck Inn, she was greeted by Abdelaziz Gren, one of the regulars. Gren was born in Morocco and came to the United States so he could live the American Dream, which included owning his own business and having his own home and car. He had learned English and attended college while living in Morocco so that he would be prepared when he arrived in the 'promised land.' He spoke fluent Arabic, English, and French. Upon arriving in America, Gren attended Old Dominion University, while working in his family's restaurant.

Everyone who knew him spoke of his big heart and how he would help anybody in need. During Thanksgiving, Gren had been taking a walk along the Lynnhaven River, where he came across a fisherman. The fisherman was taking fish below the size limit. Gren brought this to the attention of the man, who replied that he depended on his catch to feed his family.

Gren went to a local grocery store and bought food for the man and his family. He once told his sister that his altruism came from his gratitude for all the opportunities he had received since coming to this country. Gren frequently gave Clagett money so he could buy food, and would occasionally treat him to drinks at the Witchduck.

Rounds entered the kitchen where she saw Son talking to Wendel Parrish. Parrish was the tavern's cook and handyman. He was born in Prince George, Virginia, and later moved to Hampton Roads. He attended Bayside High School, where he graduated in

1981. The thirty-two-year-old Parrish would often treat Clagett to meals at the tavern.

Rounds was busy that day as the Witchduck attracted a larger crowd than normal as Son had the World Cup on the tavern's big-screen television. Later that night, the crowd emptied into the street. There were only a few patrons left, one of which was Gren. Rounds walked through the rear exit of the tavern and into the humid night air to take a break. What she did not realize was that it would be the last work break she would ever take.

When Rounds finished her break, she stepped back inside and returned to the kitchen. She saw Son and Parrish working. Right off the kitchen was a small room where Son's five-year-old son, Joshua, was sleeping. Son frequently brought Joshua to work as his wife worked.

She went back to the dining area to check on her customers when she spotted Clagett and Holsinger. Holsinger was playing pool while Clagett was at a nearby table.

Seeing Holsinger and Clagett made her uncomfortable. She had a bad feeling about Clagett. Now that Holsinger had been fired, she did not trust her, either. Little did Rounds know, she was minutes away from Virginia Beach's first quadruple murder.

As per Holsinger's plan, Clagett monitored the activity in the small tavern as Holsinger played pool. Holsinger looked at Clagett, waiting for him to make eye contact with her; their mutual eye contact was the signal to make their move. The audience for the World Cup had left along with most of the regulars. The remaining people in the tavern were Son, Parrish, Rounds, and Gren.

Holsinger gave Clagett a nod and rushed to the counter, jumping over it. She went straight for the cash register as Clagett pulled out a .357-Magnum revolver and joined her behind the counter. He ordered everyone in the restaurant to gather in the kitchen and get on the floor.

Everyone but Parrish complied. He refused to give in to the threats and remained on his barstool. Holsinger tried to get Clagett to 'do it!' Clagett hesitated. Holsinger was insistent that he comply. She repeated her order. Clagett collected his nerve, placed the barrel of his gun inches from Parrish's face and pulled the trigger.

The bullet passed through Parrish's head, and he slumped forward on the bar. Rounds screamed in terror as she lay on the floor. Son and Gren remained silent and did not move. Holsinger ordered Clagett to continue shooting the rest of them. One by one, Clagett shot each person on the floor execution-style, placing his gun to the back of their head and shooting. When he was done, the kitchen floor was covered in blood.

Holsinger grabbed four hundred dollars from the register. A small pittance for their efforts. When they were about to take off, Holsinger noticed Son's son, Joshua, sleeping in the other room. Holsinger ordered Clagett to shoot the child. Telling him they could not leave any witnesses.

Clagett could not pull the trigger on the sleeping child. Fearful of waiting for a second longer, Holsinger fled without Clagett. She drove off in their car, leaving Clagett behind. Still strung out from the drugs and alcohol from the previous two days, Clagett felt a deep sense of fear as he stared at the bloody, dead bodies. He screamed and ran out of the tavern into the dark, humid night.

At midnight, one of the regulars, Richard T. Reed, arrived at the Witchduck Inn for a drink. The Witchduck was open until two in the morning; however, Reed found the front door locked. He heard music playing inside, so he went around to the back entrance. To his surprise, the rear entrance was unlocked. Normally, the back door was locked.

Upon entering the tavern, he was met with a very bloody scene: bloodied bodies on the kitchen floor and Parrish slumped over the bar.

He called 911 and was soon joined by another regular, who was well-liked by Joshua. Joshua called the man "Uncle Richie." Knowing Joshua frequently slept at the restaurant, he ran inside.

With a singular focus, the man made his way past the dead bodies, over the blood-covered floor, and reached the room. To his relief, Joshua was unharmed but terrified. The man comforted Joshua and carried him out of the restaurant, making sure to cover his eyes.

Minutes later, Joshua was sitting in the back seat of a squad car with "Uncle Richie," who was comforting him. Both of them watched as bodies, covered by blankets, were pushed by on gurneys as first responders loaded them into the back of the waiting ambulances.

Apprehended

On July 1, 1994, Virginia Beach Police Officer Donna Malcolm was on patrol when she received a call requesting an officer respond to a disturbance. When she arrived at the address, the resident told Malcolm that a man was sleeping in the bushes of her front yard.

Malcolm arrested the man for public intoxication and brought him to police headquarters, where he was questioned by Detective Yoakum. The man Yoakum was interviewing was Clagett.

What Clagett did not know was that police had arrested Holsinger earlier. She had been pulled over for reckless driving when she had fled the crime scene. Because Holsinger provided a description of Clagett, Yoakum had a strong suspicion that the man he was talking to was the murderer; however, Clagett continued to deny any involvement with the Witchduck Inn killings.

Yoakum deceived Clagett, by telling him he had been caught by the tavern's security cameras at the time of the murders. Hearing this, Clagett stopped denying his involvement and confessed to the killings.

The police detective told Clagett that was exactly what they would be asking the court. His rant during confession: 'Fry me; I'm not gonna live. I don't want the taxpayers supporting me. I did it. Yeah, I did it. I did it all. All-by-my-fucking-self. Let that little cunt go free. I did it all. I did it all buddy. And the worst thing was Lam (Son) was my buddy!'

Later that same day, a reporter from WTKR Channel 3 news asked Clagett if he was guilty of the charges. Clagett replied to the reporter, 'Yes. I shot every one of them.'

Clagett later reversed himself by claiming that his confessions of guilt were made while he was still under the influence of drugs. He was put on trial. The ten-day trial ended with the jury finding Clagett guilty of four counts of capital murder, one count of multiple homicide capital murder, robbery, and the use of a firearm.

On October 24, 1995, Clagett was placed on death row.

A year later, Clagett married his first cousin, Karen Elaine Sparks, in a jailhouse ceremony.

On July 6, 2000, Clagett was strapped to the electric chair while some family members of the victims, Clagett's mother, and his new wife, looked on in silence. Clagett was expressionless at first, then broke down while he apologized to the victim's families.

Once he was secured in the chair, the first of two electrical charges were discharged. The first charge was eighteen hundred twenty-five volts and lasted thirty seconds, while the second charge was two hundred and forty volts for sixty seconds. He was pronounced dead after the second shock.

He would be the last person in the United States to be executed using the electric chair.

Holsinger is serving five life sentences plus twenty-three years in the Fluvanna Correctional Center for Women.

The End of **The Preview**

Visit us at **truecrimeseven.com** or scan QR Code using your phone's **camera app** to find more true crime books and other cool goodies.

About True Crime Seven

True Crime Seven is about exploring the stories of the sinful minds in this world. From unknown murderers to well-known serial killers. It is our goal to create a place for true crime enthusiasts to satisfy their morbid curiosities while sparking new ones.

Our writers come from all walks of life but with one thing in common, and that is they are all true crime enthusiasts. You can learn more about them below:

Ryan Becker is a True Crime author who started his writing journey in late 2016. Like most of you, he loves to explore the process of how individuals turn their darkest fantasies into a reality. Ryan has always had a passion for storytelling. So, writing is the best output for him to combine his fascination with psychology and true crime. It is Ryan's goal for his readers to experience the full immersion with the dark reality of the world, just like how he used to in his younger days.

Nancy Alyssa Veysey is a writer and author of true crime books, including the bestselling, Mary Flora Bell: The Horrific True Story Behind an Innocent Girl Serial Killer. Her medical degree and work in the field of forensic psychology, along with postgraduate studies in criminal justice, criminology, and pre-law, allow her to bring a unique perspective to her writing.

Kurtis-Giles Veysey is a young writer who began his writing career in the fantasy genre. In late 2018, he parlayed his love and knowledge of history into writing nonfiction accounts of true crime stories that occurred in centuries past. Told from a historical perspective, Kurtis-Giles brings these victims and their killers back to life with vivid descriptions of these heinous crimes.

Kelly Gaines is a writer from Philadelphia. Her passion for storytelling began in childhood and carried into her college career. She received a B.A. in English from Saint Joseph's University in 2016, with a concentration in Writing Studies. Now part of the real world, Kelly enjoys comic books, history documentaries, and a good scary story. In her true-crime work, Kelly focuses on the motivations of the killers and backgrounds of the victims to draw a complete picture of each individual. She deeply enjoys writing for True Crime Seven and looks forward to bringing more spine-tingling tales to readers.

James Parker, the pen-name of a young writer from New Jersey, who started his writing journey with play-writing. He has always been fascinated with the psychology of murderers and how the media might play a role in their creation. James loves to constantly test out new styles and ideas in his writing so one day he can find something cool and unique to himself.

Brenda Brown is a writer and an illustrator-cartoonist. Her art can be found in books distributed both nationally and internationally. She has also written many books related to her graduate degree in psychology and her minor in history. Like many true crime enthusiasts, she loves exploring the minds of those who see the world as a playground for expressing the darker side of themselves—the side that people usually locked up and hid from scrutiny.

Genoveva Ortiz is a Los Angeles-based writer who began her career writing scary stories while still in college. After receiving a B.A. in English in 2018, she shifted her focus to nonfiction and the real-life horrors of crime and unsolved mysteries. Together with True Crime Seven, she is excited to further explore the world of true crime through a social justice perspective.

You can learn more about us and our writers at:

https://truecrimeseven.com/about/

For updates about new releases, as well as exclusive promotions, join True Crime Seven readers' group and you can also **receive a free book today.** Thank you and see you soon.

Sign up at: **freebook.truecrimeseven.com/**

Or **scan QR Code using your phone's camera app.**

Dark Fantasies Turned Reality

Prepare yourself, we're not going to **hold back on details or cut out any of the gruesome truths...**

Printed in Great Britain
by Amazon